SKETCHING BIRDS

ISBN: 978-0-9568080-5-9

www.vicbearcroft.co.uk

Little Acorns Publishing
78 Grove Street
Balderton
Newark
Nottinghamshire
NG24 3AS
(44) 1636 651699

CONTENTS

Small Garden Birds   Page 2

Large Garden Birds   Page 8

Corvids   Page 14

Waterfowl   Page 20

Birds of Prey   Page 26

Sea Birds   Page 32

Afterword   Page 38

Introduction

Sketching, for me, is an essential part of being an artist. I see sketching as an extension of doodling, and a gateway to more 'complete' artworks. Regular sketching will also help to hone your drawing skills, in the same way as daily practice of scales on a piano will make you a better musician.

Sketching helps to forge a link between what we see and what we create with a pencil on a blank sheet of paper.

Full sketchbooks, containing even basic sketches or doodles, are like journals, full of visual memories and information to look back on.

Above all, sketching should be a stress-free and fun activity.

Regardless of how much sketching you already do, I hope that this book, which shows you some of my favourite techniques, will inspire and encourage you to do more.

About the book

The chapters in this book cover six groups of birds. They are not separated by genus, species or subspecies, rather by my own general, non-scientific grouping.
Within each chapter there is an 'essential features' section which focuses on aspects pertaining to that particular group of birds; features such as beaks/bills, feet, etc.

There is also a step-by-step sketching project, focussing on one member of that group. These all start with simple shapes that anyone can do; circles, ovals and triangles.

I hope you will have a go at the tutorials and perhaps use the techniques to sketch other birds.

Materials

All my own sketches, including those in this book, are created using:

- 2B graphite pencil
- 130gsm or 150gsm cartridge paper
- kneadable eraser
- Paper blenders (tortillons) or paper towel.

CHAPTER 1

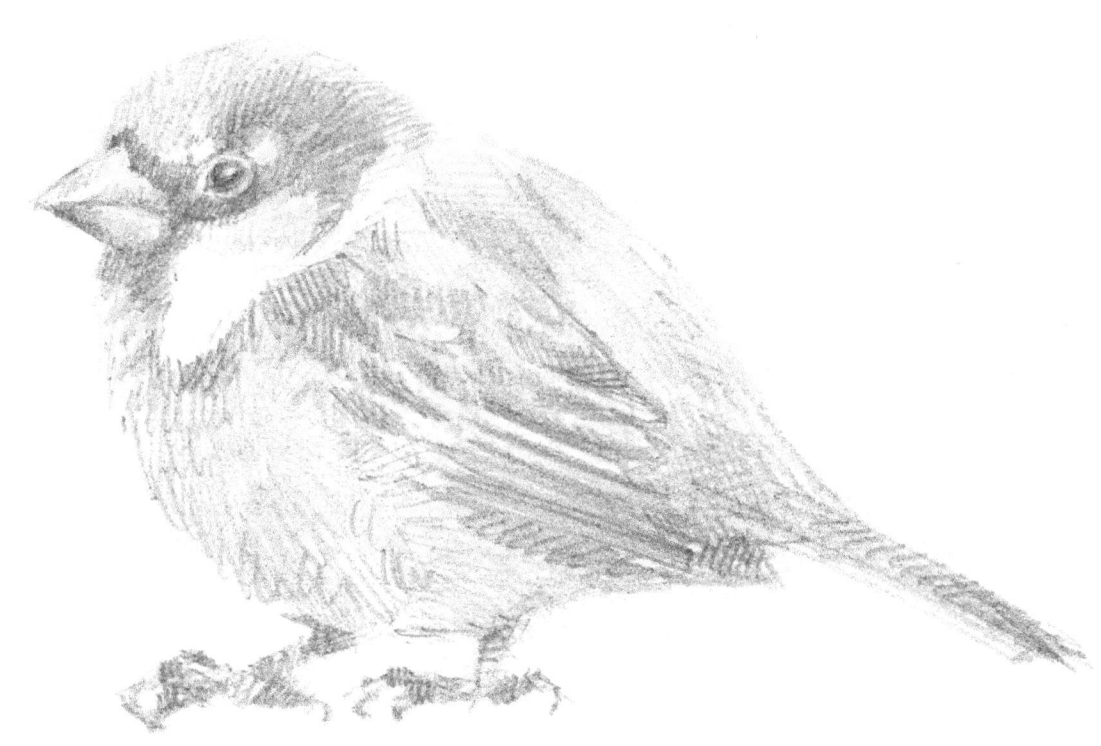

SMALL GARDEN BIRDS

SMALL GARDEN BIRDS

The birds in this group are those which we are most likely to see feeding or nesting in our gardens on a regular basis; the small *Passeriformes* (sparrow-like birds) which includes more than half the world's bird species.

I would include such birds as sparrows, dunnocks, robins and tits in this group, as they generally share similar attributes.

ESSENTIAL FEATURES

Beak/Bill

The terms 'beak' and 'bill' are applicable to all birds, both air and waterborne. However since I, like many others, have always thought of waterfowl as having a bill and sparrows, pigeons, etc. as having beaks, then I'll continue with those descriptions herein. Our small garden birds are happy eating a variety of foods, from seeds to insects, so their beaks are adapted accordingly. Short, sharp, strong beaks can easily pick up small insects as well as being able to crack and discard the less digestible husks from seeds. Here is a typical 'Passeriformes' beak.

Feet

Another attribute that birds in this group have in common is that they are all perching birds; their feet adapted to gripping tightly onto branches. Their feet have three front facing toes and one rear facing. From the inner toe outwards there are two, three and four toe bones (phalanges), and one on the hind toe. Note in the illustration that the knee joint (patella) is hidden from view, so that the part of the leg/foot that we normally see is from just below the knee down.

Wings

Broadly speaking, there are three types of feather on a bird's wing – primary flight feathers (long and pointed), secondary flight feathers (more rounded/squared ends) and coverts, which, as the name suggests, cover the leading edge of the wing.

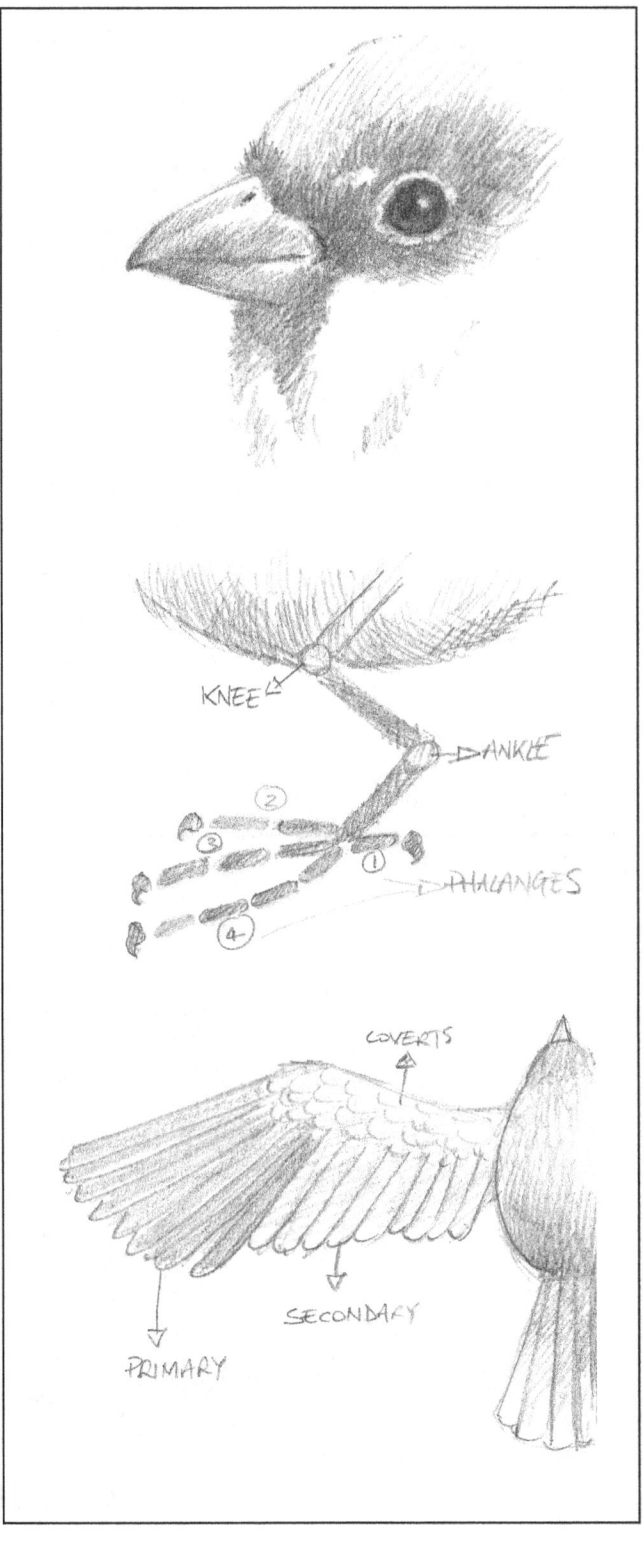

PROJECT

Male house sparrow *(passer domesticus)*

Most of us are familiar with these gregarious little brown birds that hang around our urban and suburban gardens eating most anything they can find.

Unfortunately they are not as common as they used to be and have been in decline by as much as 70% since the 1970s, which is a shame as they are good at helping to dispose of our food rubbish and wastefulness.

There is a visual difference between the male and female house sparrow. The female is mostly shades of brown and grey, while the male has distinct black, grey and white markings around the head.

Despite the decline in numbers, the house sparrow also happens to be the most widely distributed wild bird.

In ancient Egypt these little birds were believed to capture the souls of the dead, carrying them into the afterlife.

 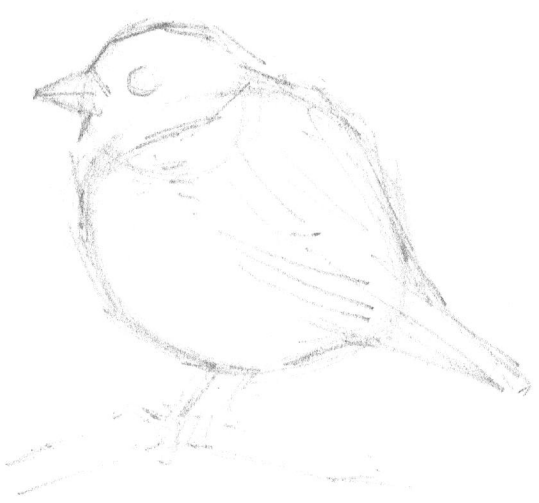

STEP 1

Begin by drawing a circle to represent the head, followed by a rounded oval/egg shape for the small, rounded body. These two shapes should overlap as our sparrow doesn't have much of a visible neck.
Draw a small circle for the eye, close to and lining up with the beak, which is a small wide-based triangle that forms the basis of the sparrow's short, sharp beak.

STEP 2

I always find the easiest and most dynamic way to sketch curves is to break them down into straight lines and angles. You can see how the head, neckline and chest appear to have a strong sense of form that would be lacking if I had carefully drawn or traced the outline.

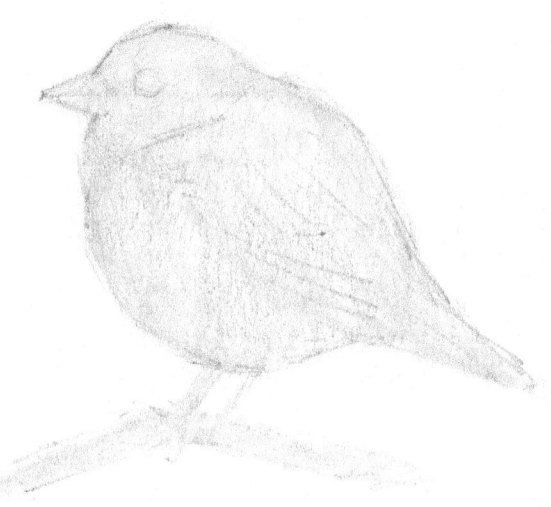

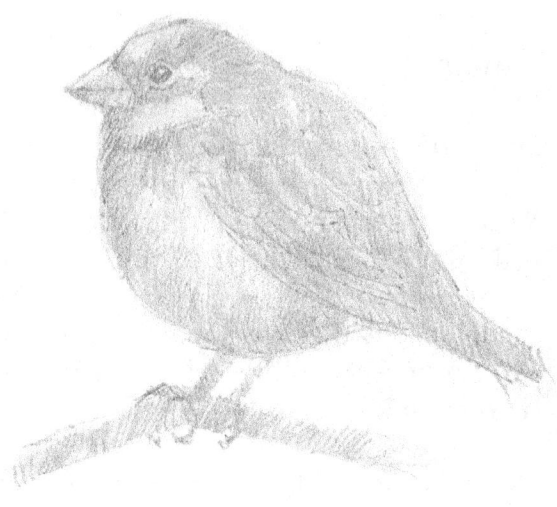

STEP 3

Using the side of the pencil, lay down a mid-grey overall tone that can be used as a foundation to be added to, as well as lifted out. Gently blend and soften the pencil shading with a tortillon or rolled up sheet of paper towel.
You can then use a kneadable eraser to clean up around the edges.

STEP 4

Begin to add some textures and details, but try not to get carried away with the details; you're not trying to create a scientifically correct illustration.
Loosely define the wing feathers from shoulder coverts to secondary flight feathers to primaries.
Use short, hatching strokes to suggest the smaller (contour) feathers that cover most of the body away from the wings and tail feathers.
If you want to, you can soften this first textured layer by firmly stroking over the pencil hatching (not rubbing) with a tortillon.

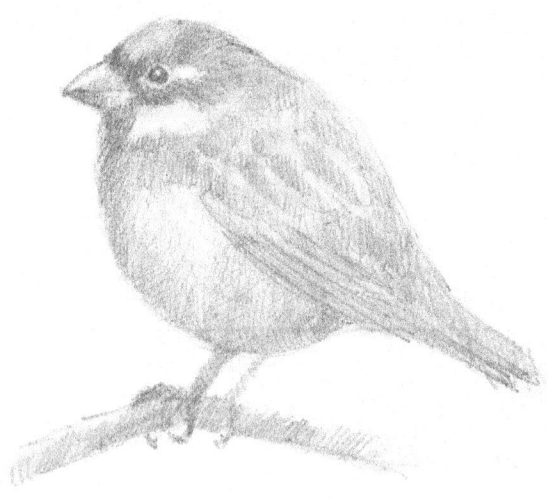

STEP 5

Final details can now be added to bolster areas of the sketch that you consider important.
Adding sharper details in the beak and around the eyes, as well as darkening them, will focus the viewer's attention to this area.
Use the kneadable eraser to lift out pale feathers and highlights at the end to keep them fresh.

A LITTLE BIRD TOLD ME...

If you want to make your sketch look like part of a nature journal, do a little research on your house sparrow and embellish the image with notes, side sketches (remarques), and decorative borders.

ADDITIONAL SMALL GARDEN BIRD IMAGES

ROBIN

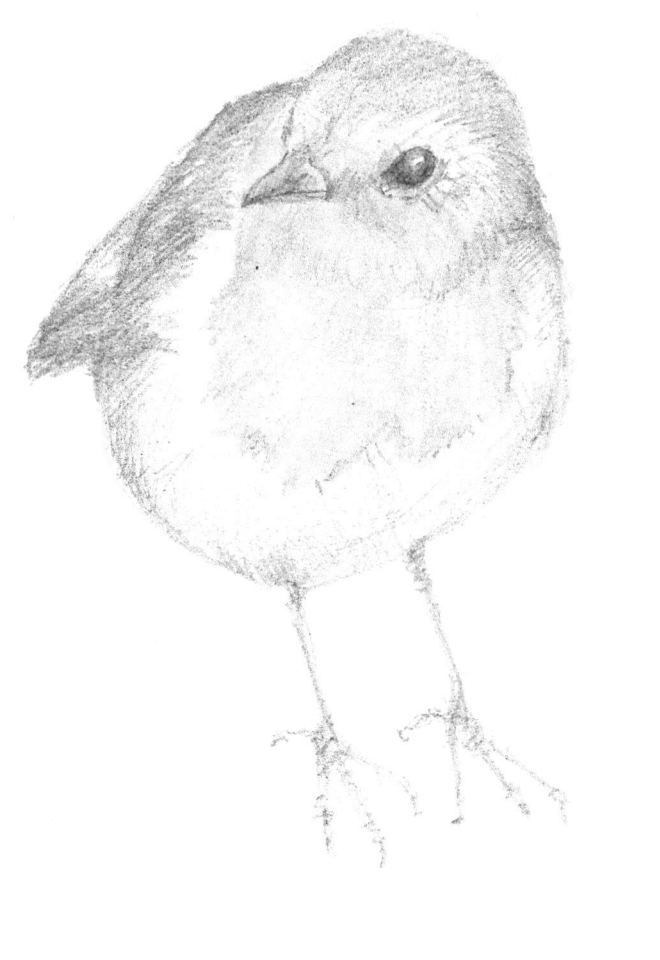

BLUE TIT

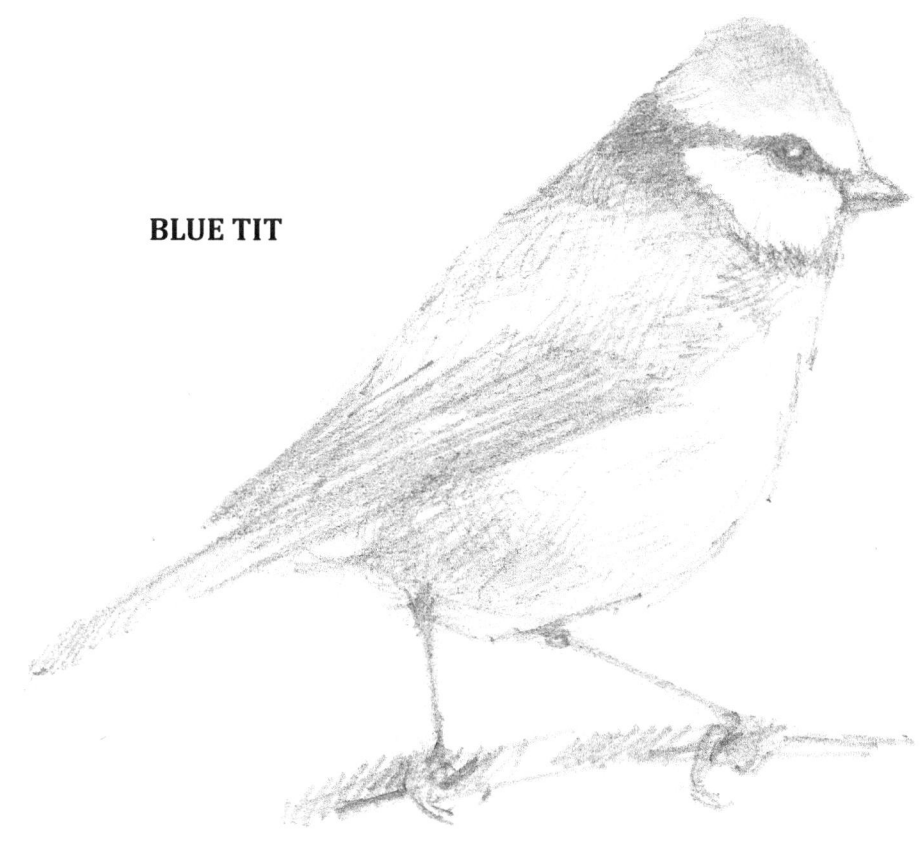

WHO KILLED COCK ROBIN?

MOST WIDELY DISTRIBUTED WILD BIRD ACROSS THE GLOBE

71% DECLINE SINCE 1977 IN UK

SOCIAL & GREGARIOUS

ANCIENT EGYPTIANS BELIEVED THAT SPARROWS CAUGHT THE SOULS OF THOSE WHO DIED & CARRIED THEM INTO THE AFTERLIFE

SHORT, SHARP BEAK, FOR CRACKING HUSKS

DIET: SEEDS & SCRAPS

HOUSE SPARROW

ASSOCIATED WITH HUMAN HABITATION

PASSER DOMESTICUS

"PASSER" = SPARROW
"FORMIS" = SHAPED

1. SIMPLE SHAPES
2. LINES & ANGLES
3. BASE TONE
4. DETAILS & TEXTURES
5. HIGHLIGHTS

CHAPTER 2

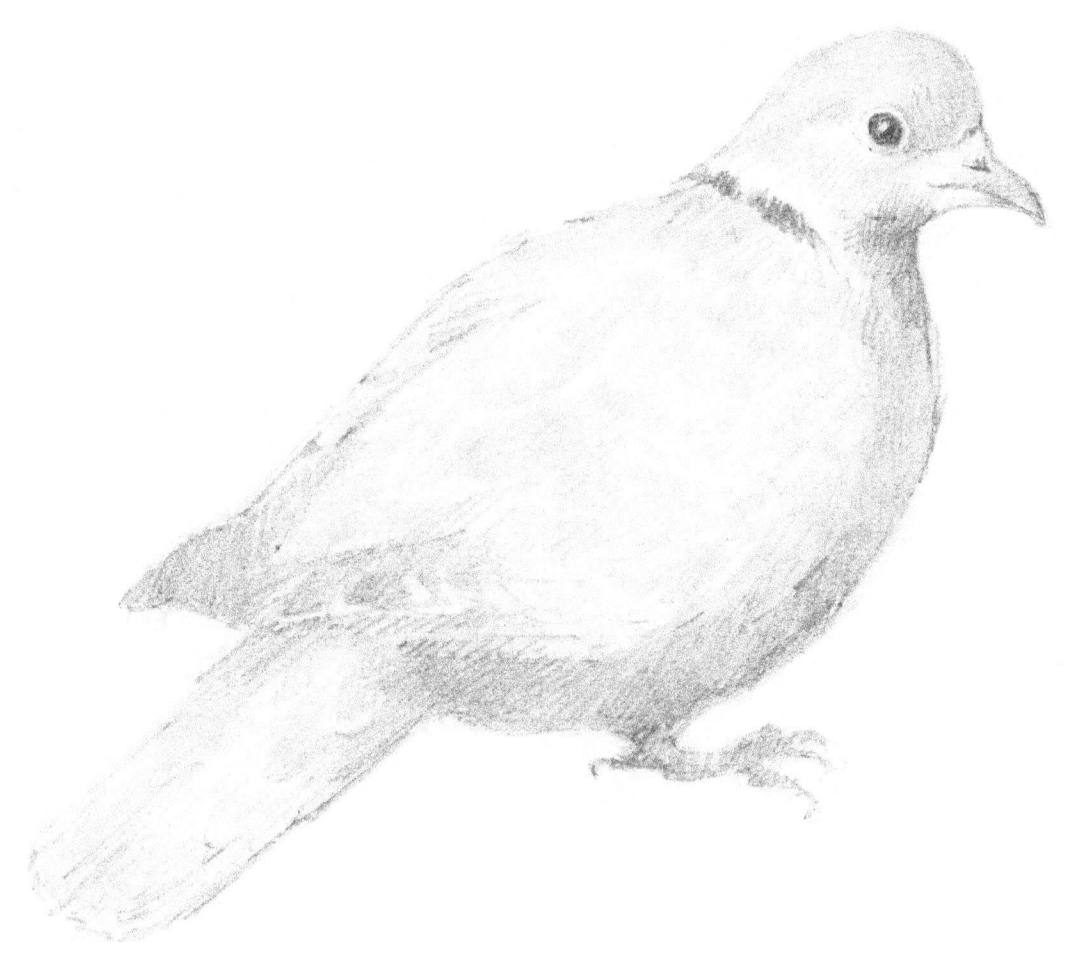

LARGE GARDEN BIRDS

LARGE GARDEN BIRDS

I have categorised this group as being those birds that might visit your garden occasionally, providing there is a suitable food source, even if that food is supplied by you in the form of fruit and berry-bearing trees and bushes, or by putting out seeds and nuts, suet pellets and mealworms.

My contenders for this group would therefore be wood pigeons, collared doves, blackbirds, starlings and, perhaps, the occasional thrush.

Large garden birds are still classified as Passeriformes, so that their eyes, wings and feet have the same basic structural shapes as the house sparrow.However, there may be some differences elsewhere.

ESSENTIAL FEATURES

Beak/Bill

Some of the large garden birds share a similar diet to their smaller neighbours, but may well have a different approach to eating. Pigeons and doves, for example, swallow seeds whole and therefore have no need for the short, strong husk-cracking beak of the sparrow.
Instead, their beaks are more suited for collecting and swallowing, as well as being used like a straw to suck up water.

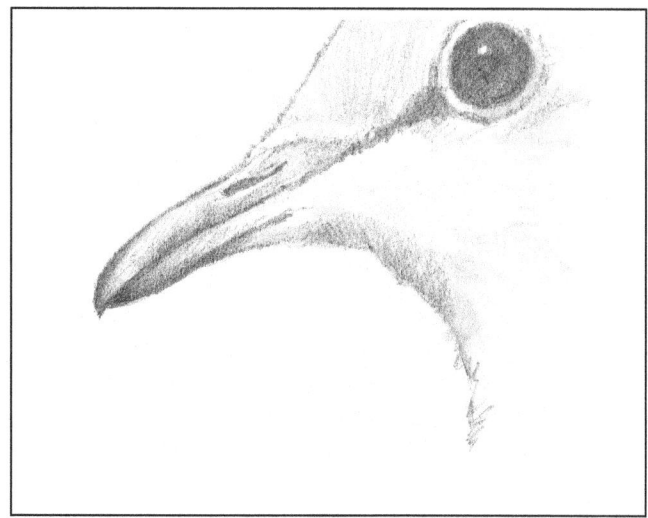

PROJECT

Collared dove *(streptopeliadecaocto)*

Long seen as a symbol of love and faithfulness, doves are monogamous and capable of breeding at any time of the year, raising their young on, rather than in the flimsiest of nests.

The second part of the scientific name – *decaocto* – translates from the Greek as 'ten eight'. This refers to a Greek fable about an overworked servant girl who was underpaid (18 pieces a year). The gods turned her into a dove so that she could escape her misery. The dove's call is said to sound like the mournful cries of her former life.

With an overall grey-buff colouring, the collared dove is so named because of the black half collar, edged with white around its neck. Male and female collared doves look the same, while juveniles take some time to develop their collars.

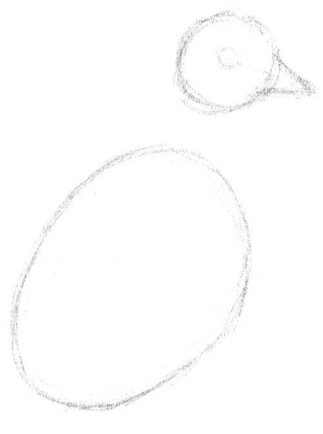

STEP 1

Begin by loosely sketching the basic shapes; a circle for the head and an oval (larger than the sparrow) for the body. Leave a gap between head and body to allow for a longer neck than the smaller garden birds.

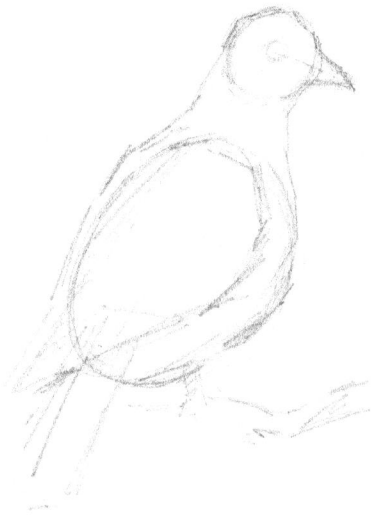

STEP 2

Use straight lines and angles to develop the overall shape, including the wing and tail feathers. The triangle for the beak is longer than that of the sparrow. Note the position of the eye – roughly in the centre of the head circle.
I have also added the suggestion of a branch for the dove to perch on.

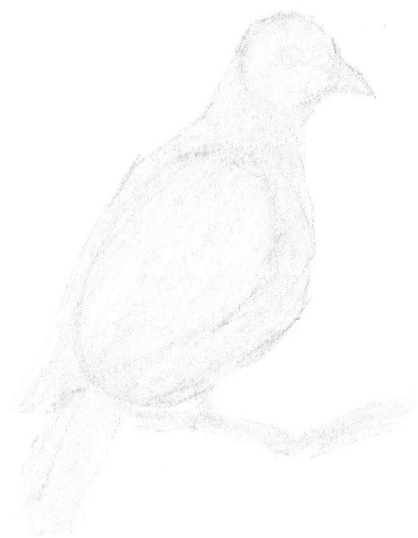

STEP 3

After erasing any unwanted lines and tidying up the outline with a kneadable eraser, use the side of the pencil lead to lay down a mid grey foundation tone. Even out and soften this tone with a tortillon or paper towel.

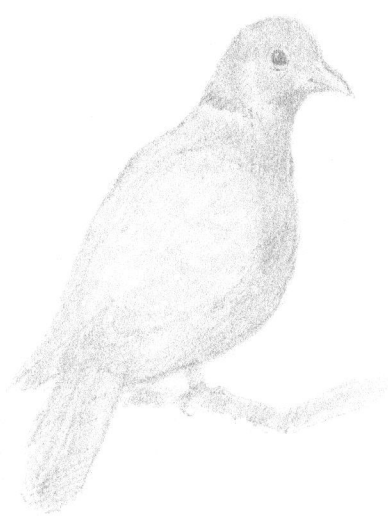

STEP 4

Begin to add textures and some details, firstly shaping the beak and the eye. The collar and shorter contour feathers are created with simple directional hatch shading; adding more layers to darken specific areas. The shapes of the various wing feathers are created with simple lines, hatch shading and kneadable eraser.

10

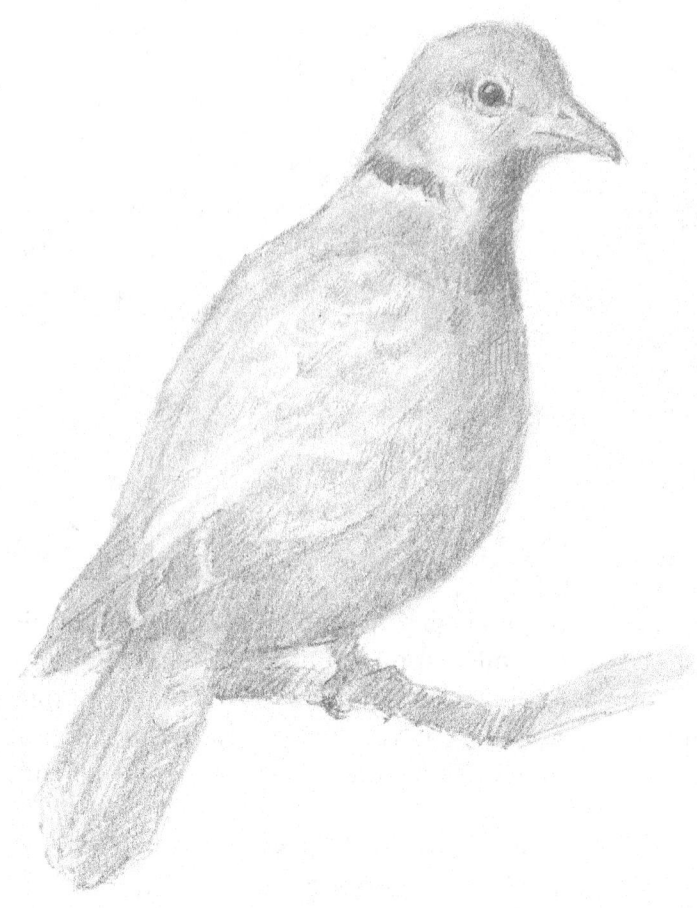

STEP 5

Review your sketch and make sure that areas that you consider important are slightly more detailed, with stronger tones. These are usually, although not exclusively, the head and features.

A LITTLE BIRD TOLD ME...

Select a suitable background for your sketch; a simple softened darker tone will push the dove forward visually. If you prefer, you can add some leaves to the branch and maybe continue that as a border for your sketch.

ADDITIONAL LARGE GARDEN BIRD IMAGES

THRUSH

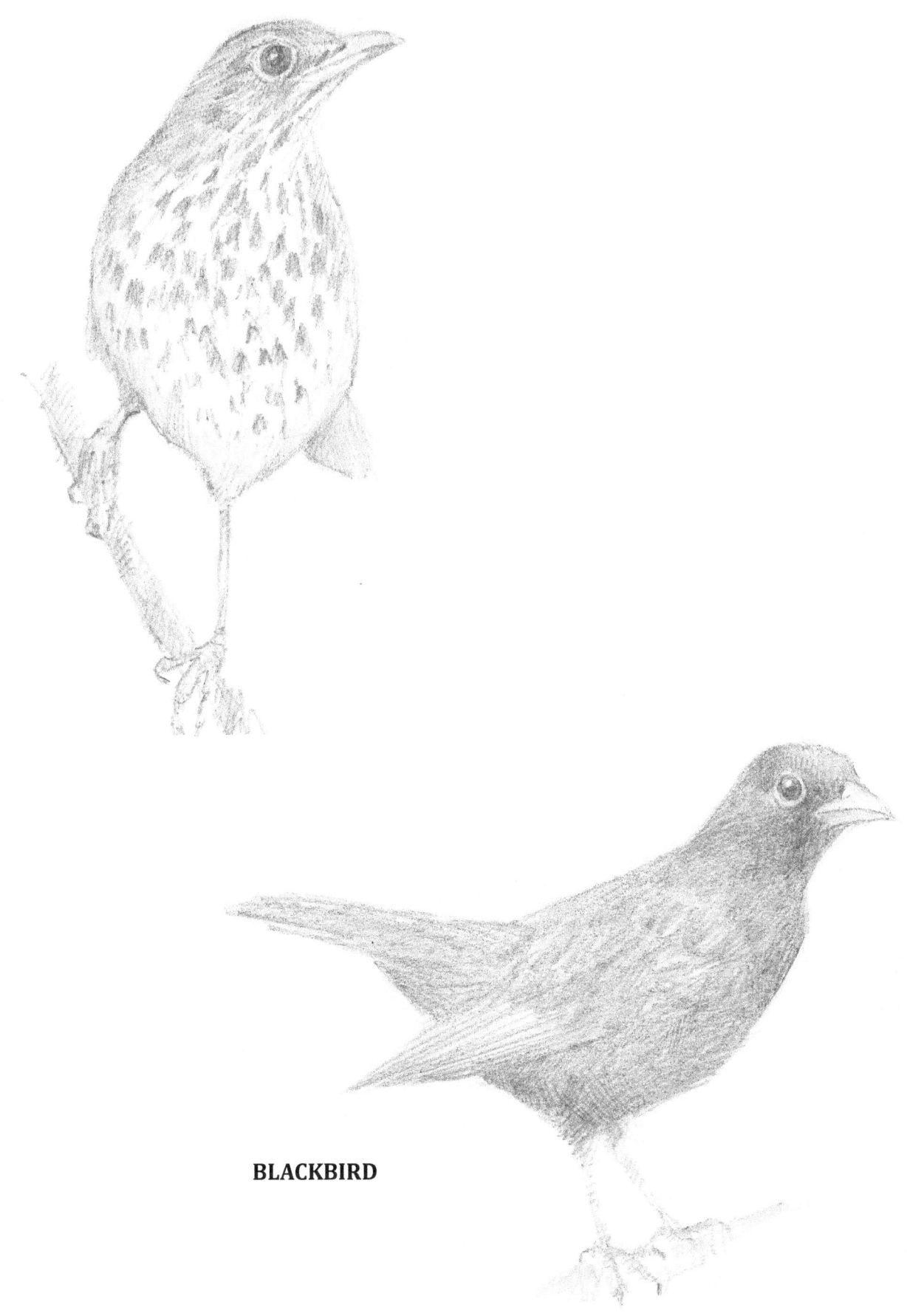

BLACKBIRD

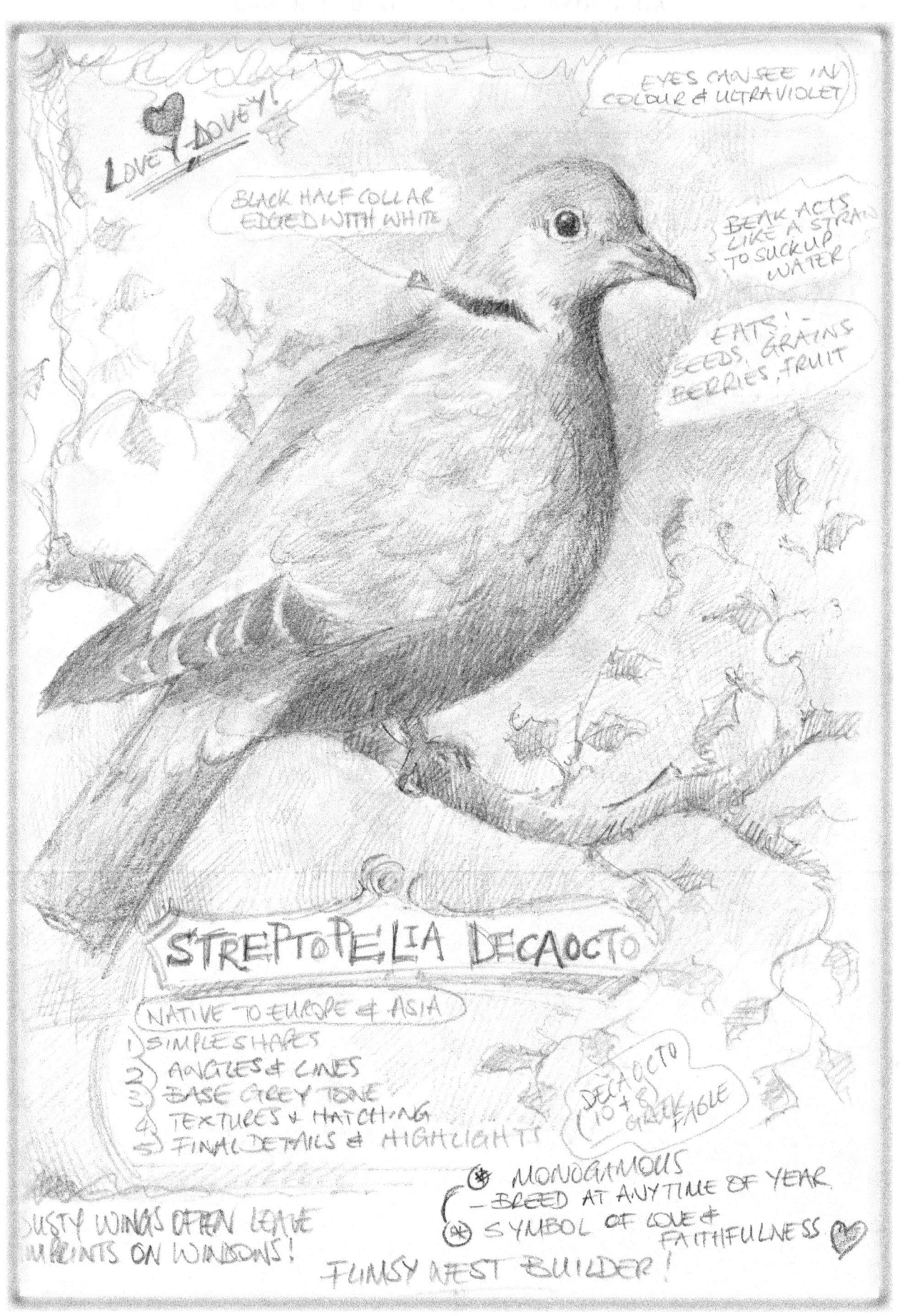

CHAPTER 3

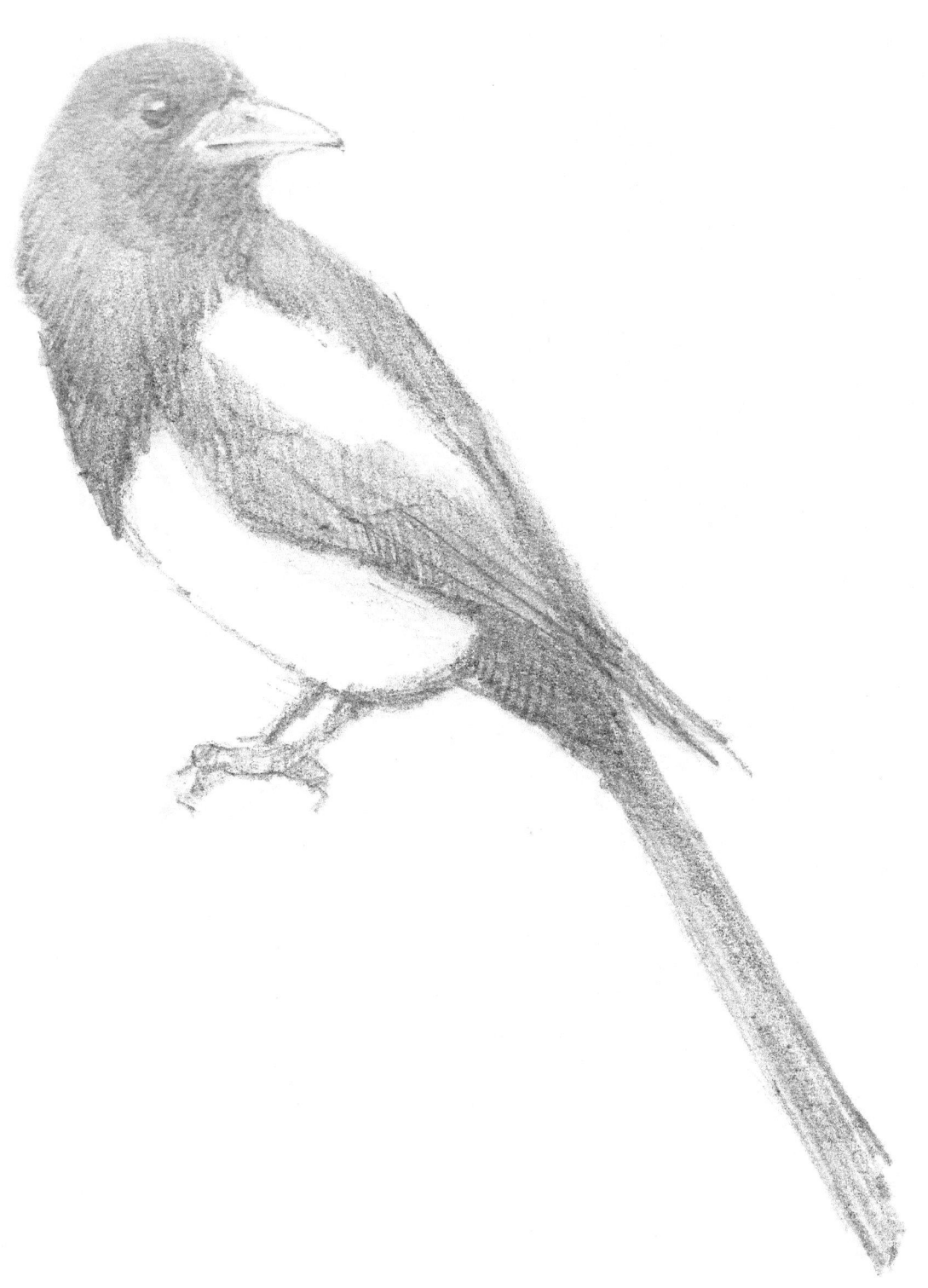

CORVIDS

CORVIDS

Possibly my favourite group, as it includes some of the most intelligent animals on the planet; crows, rooks, ravens, magpies, jackdaws and jays.

It is unlikely that you will see many of these birds in your garden, but most are relatively easy to spot on walks in the countryside or in town and city parks.

Corvids are mostly thought of as raiders and scavengers but, love them or hate them, there is no doubt that they are some of the world's most recognisable and written about birds.

ESSENTIAL FEATURES

Beak/Bill
As corvids are primarily, although not exclusively, meat eaters, they naturally have a differently designed beak than the seed and insect eaters, one that is better suited to tearing meat – long and pointed.

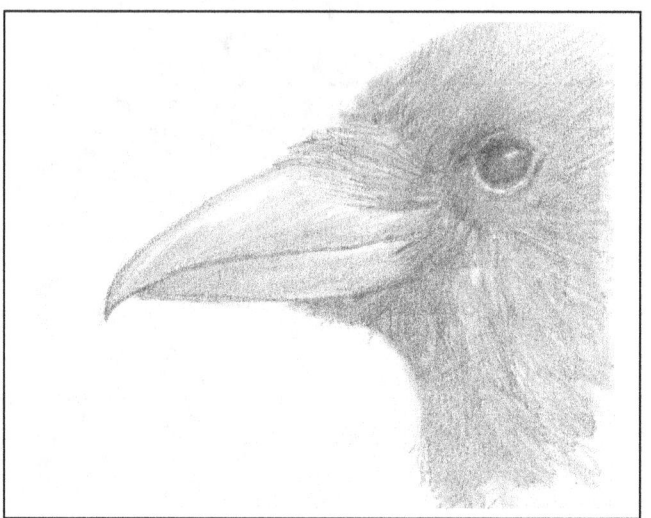

PROJECT

Eurasian Magpie *(pica pica)*.

Magpies are reputed to be one of the world's most intelligent animals; perhaps even the most intelligent after humans. Yet they seem to have been admired and reviled in equal measures throughout history.

There are so many stories, myths and superstitions surrounding magpies that they could probably fill a book by themselves.

Magpies will eat virtually anything, and their Latin name (pica pica) reflects this. Pica translates as a craving to eat anything, and the Old English name was Maggie-Pie, as it was customary to give birds names, such as Robin Redbreast, Jenny Wren, etc. The 'pie' part is an adaptation of 'pica'.

Magpies are attractive birds with their black and white plumage and long tail feathers. The black feathers shine blue-turquoise in the light.

There is more information about magpies in the finished sketch, but feel free to do more research yourself.

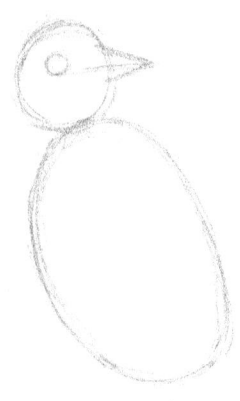

STEP 1

Begin as usual with the essential basic shapes, a circle for the head, resting on a rugby ball shaped oval. A long triangle for the beak and eye placed roughly in the centre of the circle.

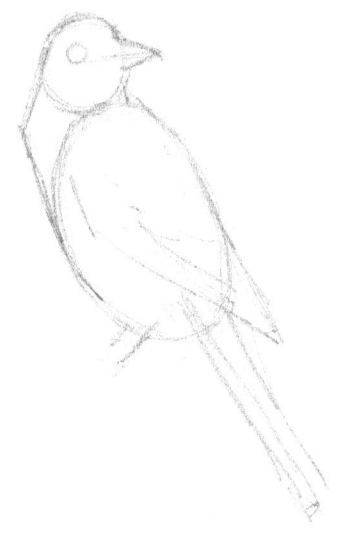

STEP 2

Use as many straight lines and angles as you can to create the outline, including the wing, long tail feathers and legs.

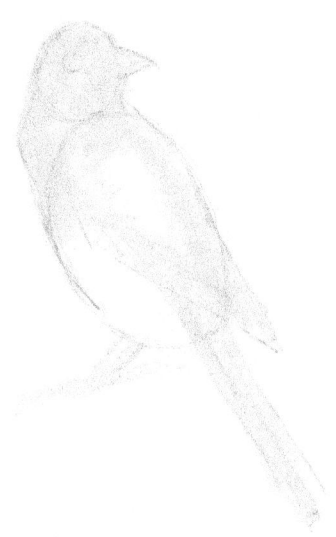

STEP 3

Lay down the mid-grey base tone where the black feathers are, blending and softening with a tortillon or paper towel.

STEP 4

Begin texturing with simple hatching strokes for the black contour feathers. It is better to add more layers to make an area darker than to press hard with your pencil; that way you'll create the impression of lots of plumage.

Roughly mark out the layers of wing feathers and hatch diagonally over the black wing and tail feathers, softening the texture just a little with the tortillon.

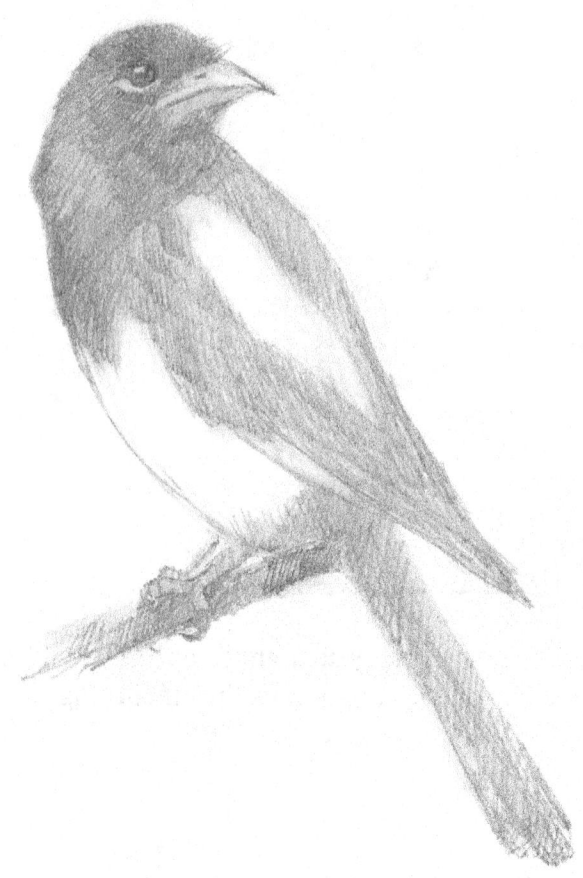

STEP 5

Carefully shape the long pointed beak, adding tone and softening as needed. You can add appropriate highlights on the shiny black beak with the kneadable eraser.

Create the shiny dark eye with just a hint of the lower rim showing. Don't forget to add a mischievous glint and darken any black plumage around the eye to create a focal point in the sketch.

A LITTLE BIRD TOLD ME...

Add some background/foreground elements of your choice or create a journal page illustration with interesting notes and remarques about this exceptional bird.

JACKDAW

CROW

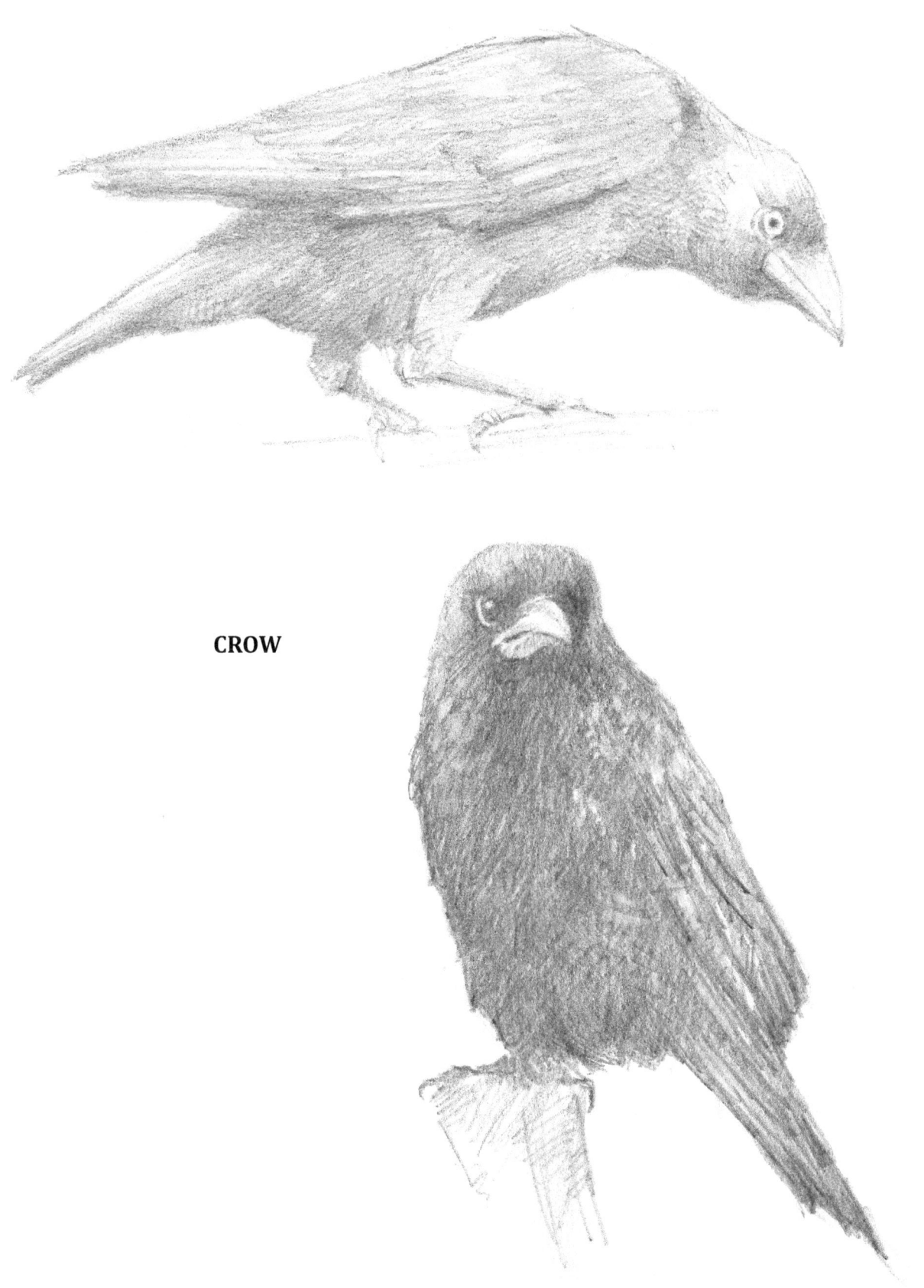

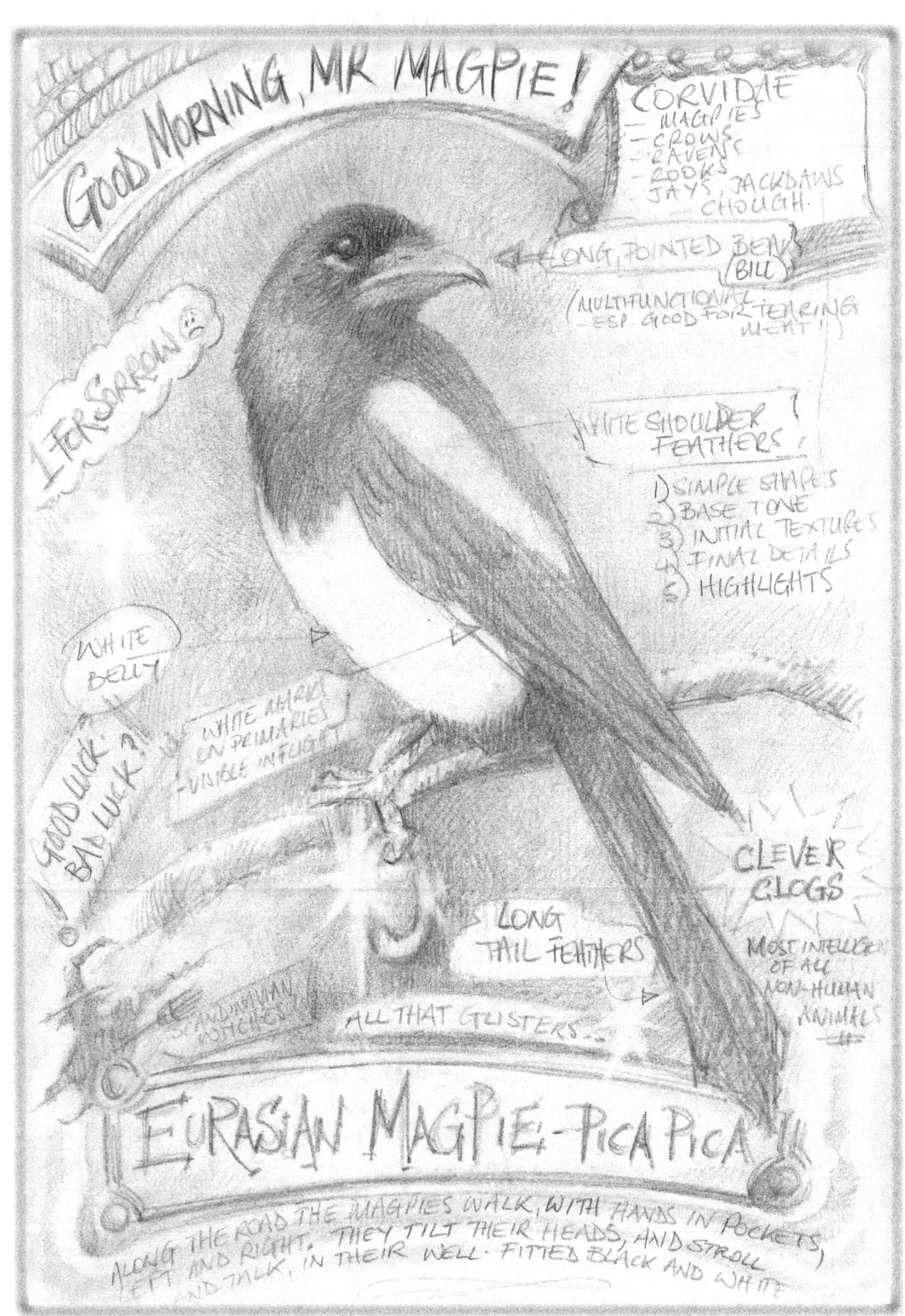

CHAPTER 4

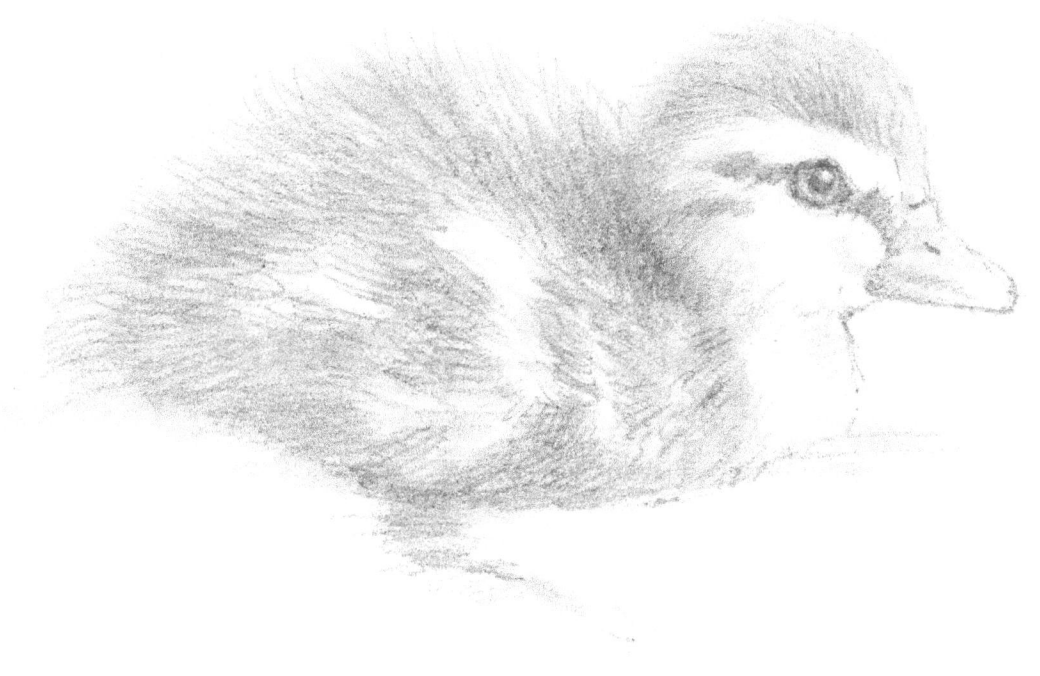

WATERFOWL

WATERFOWL

The largest family in the order of birds we call waterfowl is *anatidae*, which includes those we are most familiar with – ducks, geese and swans. In general, these birds are strong swimmers and most have webbed feet; a notable exception being moorhens who, despite the lack of webbing, still manage a fair rate of knots on our nearby lake.

The bill is designed to grab and swallow food in one gulp.It has a nail-like hook or *bean* at the tip for pulling and soft edges to help filter out water.

Webbed feet serve as paddles, but are not suited for perching, so most waterfowl waddle or stand flat-footed when out of the water.

ESSENTIAL FEATURES

Beak/Bill

Side and front views of a duck's bill showing the 'bean' at the tip.

Feet

The webbing is stretched between the first and second and the second and third toes.

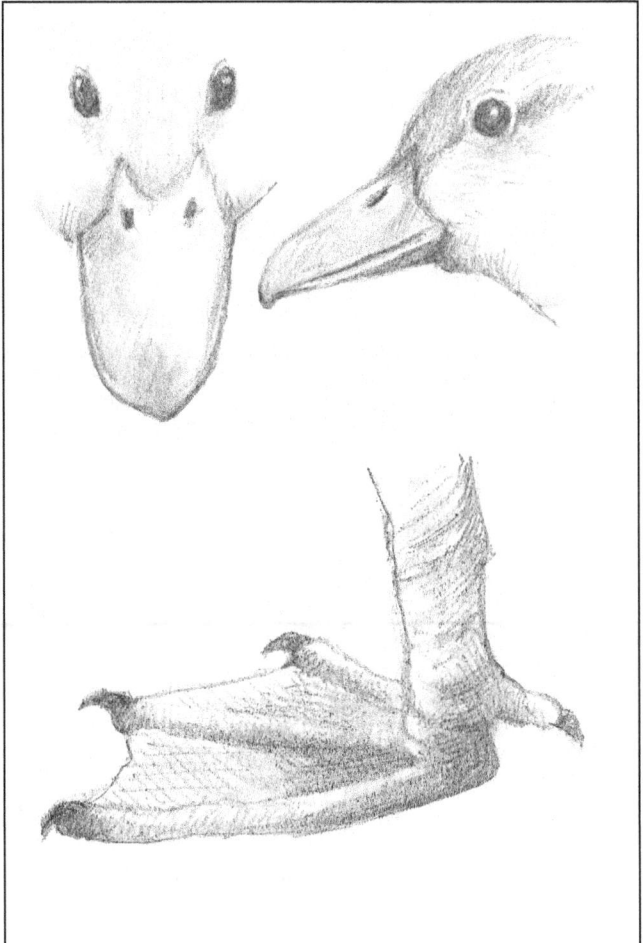

PROJECT

Mallard duckling *(anas platyrhynchos)*

Many of us have fed or still feed the ducks on our local ponds and waterways, and the one we probably know more than any other is the mallard, the main ancestor of most domestic duck breeds.

The mallard is part of the 'dabbling duck' group, which feeds mainly by upending to reach vegetation, as opposed to 'diving ducks' which have larger feet for propelling themselves down in deeper water. The cutely named 'puddle ducks' feed on the water surface or from very shallow water bottoms. The not-such-ugly-ducklings are also very skilled at catching flies.

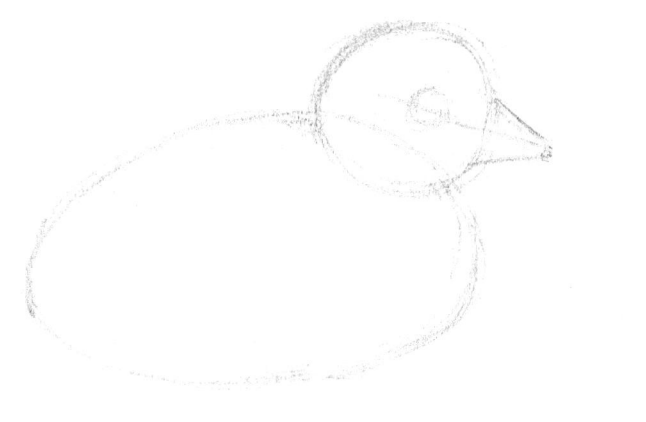 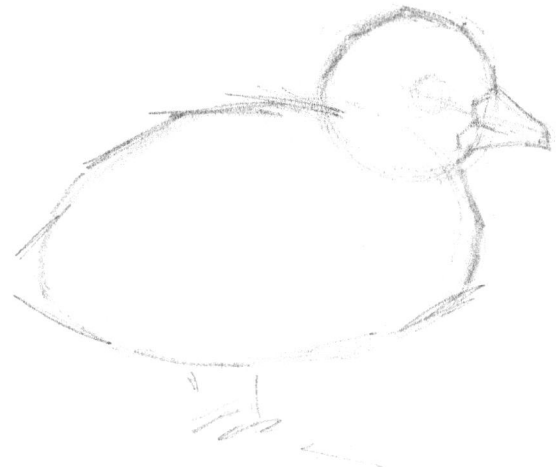

STEP 1

Begin with the simple shapes – a circle for the head, oval for the body and triangle for the bill. Note the size of the head compared to the body, which still has some catching up to do growth-wise. Also, the oval body shape is flattened a little to suggest the water level.

STEP 2

Try as much as possible to break the curves down into lines and angles. This will make the outline stronger and, once you are practised and quicker, will add energy to your sketch.

Note that the eye sits on the line that cuts the circle in half and the leg is merely a loose scribble to suggest the refraction of the water.

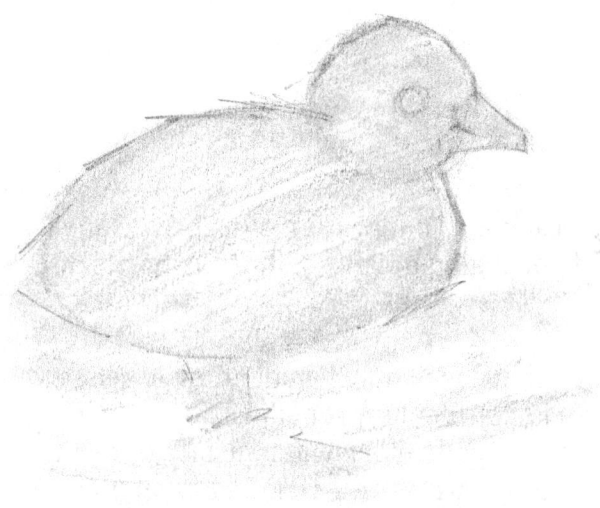

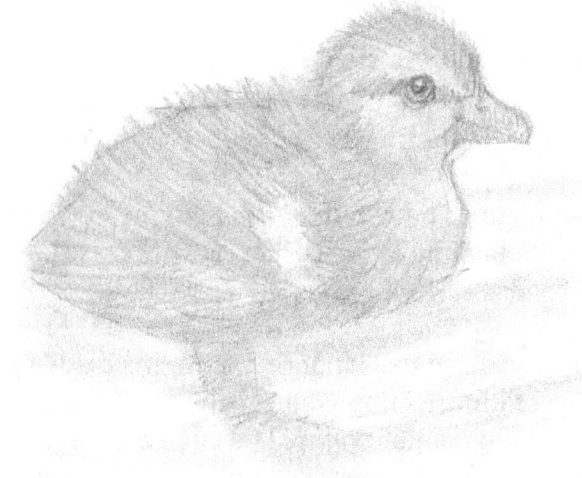

STEP 3

Add a mid grey base tone with the side of the pencil, ensuring the hatch strokes are close together if you want a smooth, even tone when you blend through with the tortillon or paper towel.
You can use the graphite-loaded tortillon to 'paint' the shape of the ripples in the water around the duckling.

STEP 4

Use hatch shading to add tone to the bill – softening the texture with the tortillon. Directional hatching will be sufficient to show the soft, downy feathers of the duckling. Overlay with more hatching for darker areas; softening a little between layers if needed.
Begin detailing the eye and dark areas around the eye. Note that the iris is slightly lighter in tone than the pupil, giving the eye a soft, appealing look. Add some tone in the backround if you'd like, or you can keep the sketch more simple by leaving it as bare paper.

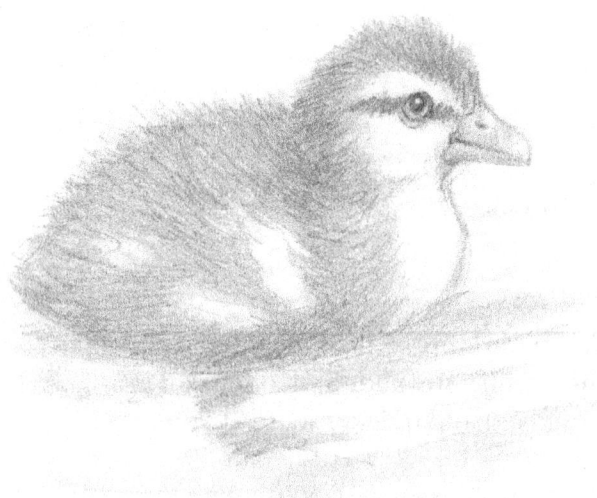

STEP 5

Add final details and highlights, ensuring that the important features are tonally stronger and more detailed.
Lift out soft highlights on the bill and paler feathers with a softened kneadable eraser. If you want to enhance the water ripples, use the eraser to lift out the reflections.

A LITTLE BIRD TOLD ME...

Once you get to this stage, you can decide to leave your duckling as a simple sketch, or add the suggestion of a pond or lake background – perhaps with a few flies for the little one to catch!

MOORHEN

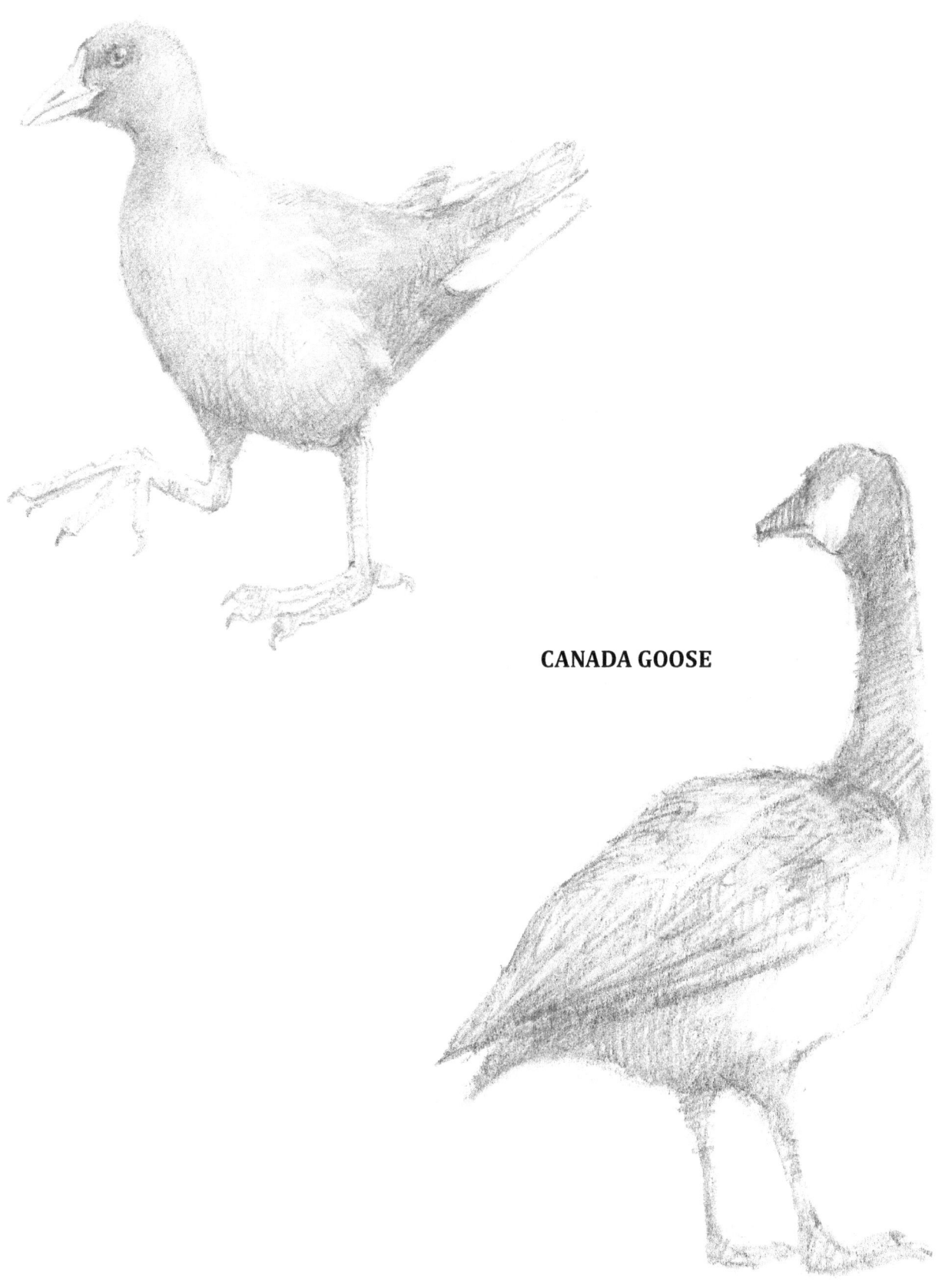

CANADA GOOSE

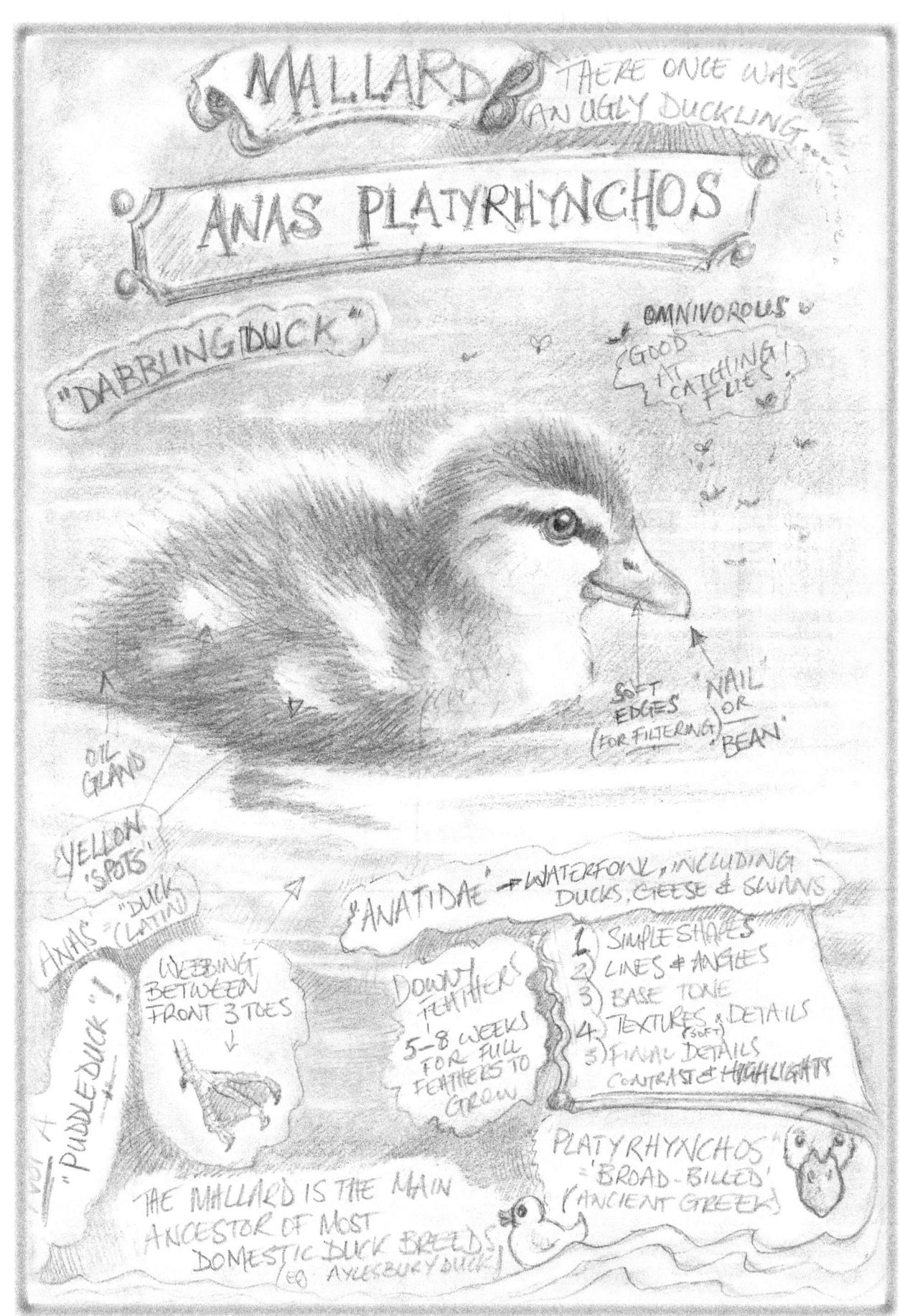

MALLARD & THERE ONCE WAS AN UGLY DUCKLING...

ANAS PLATYRHYNCHOS

"DABBLING DUCK"

OMNIVOROUS - GOOD AT CATCHING FLIES!

SOFT EDGES (FOR FILTERING) 'NAIL' OR 'BEAN'

OIL GLAND

YELLOW 'SPOTS'

ANAS = "DUCK" (LATIN)

NOT A "PUDDLE DUCK"!

WEBBING BETWEEN FRONT 3 TOES ↓

'ANATIDAE' = WATERFOWL, INCLUDING DUCKS, GEESE & SWANS

DOWN FEATHERS

5-8 WEEKS FOR FULL FEATHERS TO GROW

1. SIMPLE SHAPES
2. LINES & ANGLES
3. BASE TONE
4. TEXTURES & DETAILS (SOFT)
5. FINAL DETAILS CONTRAST & HIGHLIGHTS

THE MALLARD IS THE MAIN ANCESTOR OF MOST DOMESTIC DUCK BREEDS (EG. AYLESBURY DUCK)

PLATYRHYNCHOS 'BROAD-BILLED' (ANCIENT GREEK)

CHAPTER 5

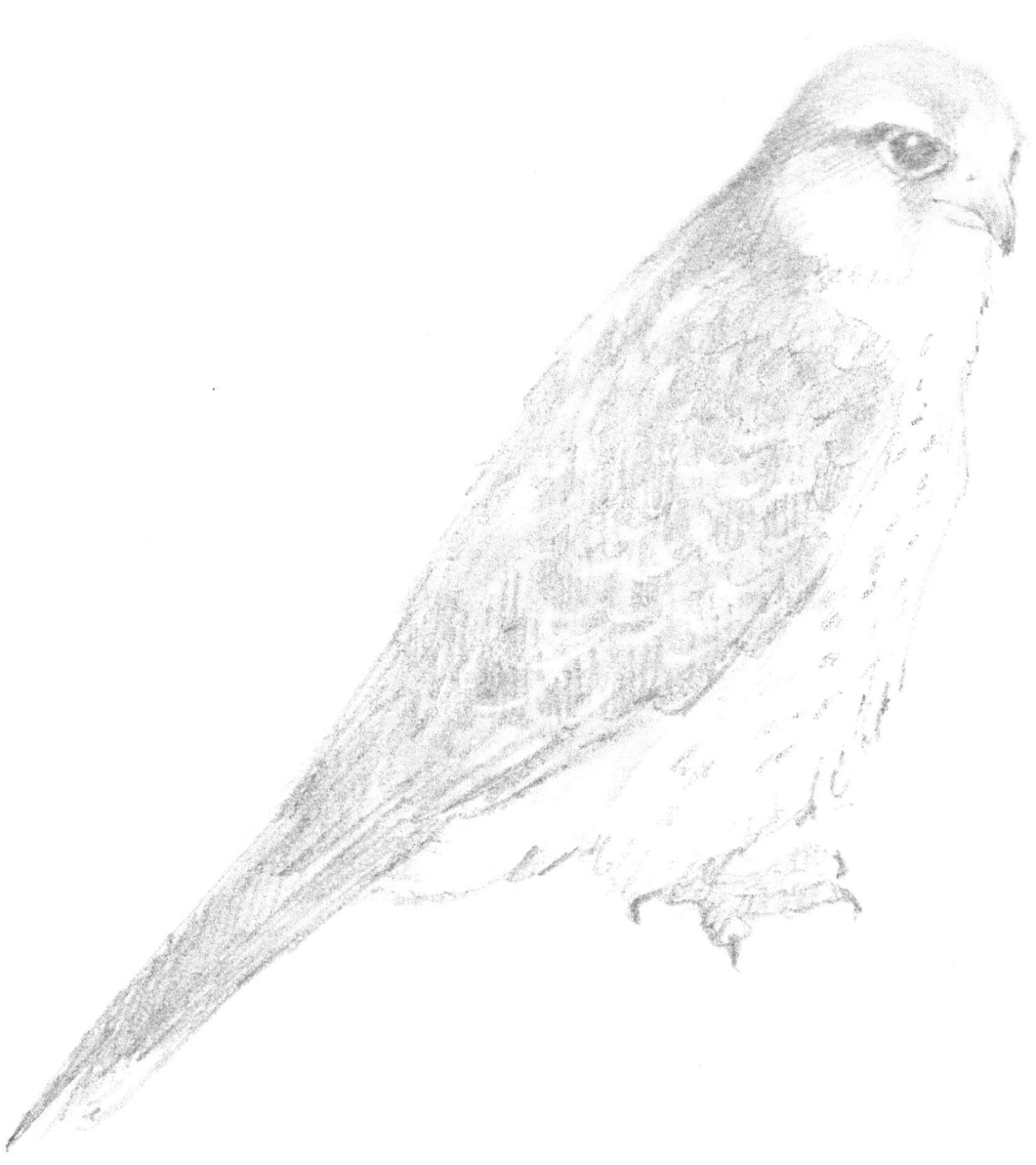

BIRDS OF PREY

BIRDS OF PREY

Birds of prey (raptors) are carnivores that hunt and feed on other vertebrates. This group includes eagles, hawks, falcons and owls.

What these raptors have in common are sharp, curved beaks, powerful talons and very keen eyesight.

You may well see at least one raptor in your garden occasionally – the sparrow hawk. Others you might be lucky see on a walk in the country; barn owls early in the morning or at dusk, buzzards circling up high, or kestrels hovering above fields.

ESSENTIAL FEATURES

Beak/Bill

Raptors' beaks are strong and curved, ending in sharp points which are ideal for tearing meat.

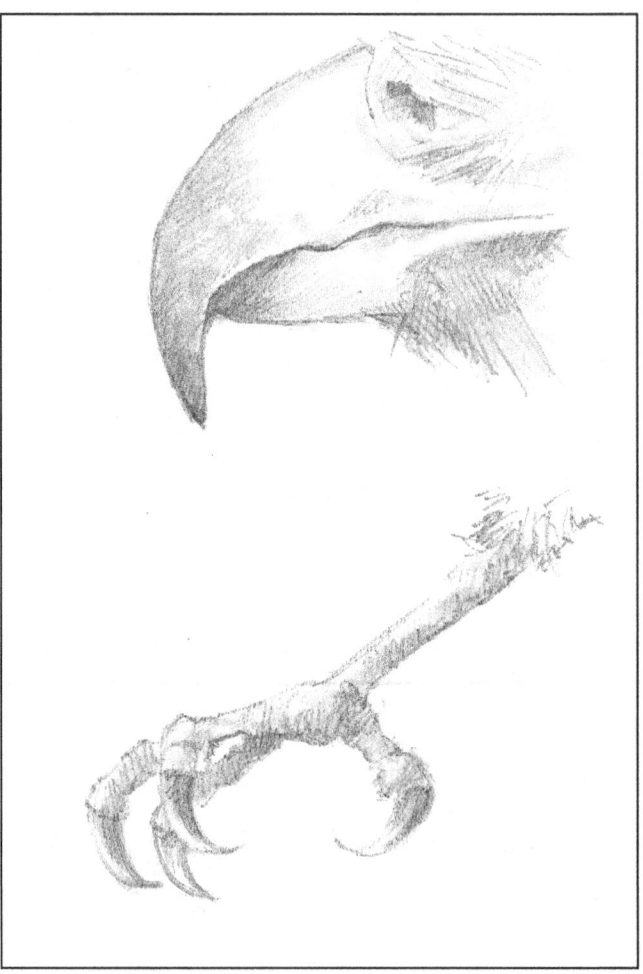

Feet

Birds of prey's feet have much the same arrangement as *passerformes,* three toes pointing forward and one pointing backward. The obvious difference to those of a sparrow are the claws, which are longer, stronger and sharper.
Whereas sparrows and other *passerformes*use their feet solely for perching, raptors also use them for catching their food.

PROJECT

Project: Kestrel *(falco tinnunculus)*.

Kestrels can easily be spotted if you know where to look.

If you're driving along motorways or any other road with fields either side, and you spot a bird hovering, almost motionless, then you are likely to have seen a kestrel. Their eyesight is so sharp that they can spot a beetle from 50 yards away.

Unlike owls, which, if you're lucky, can be seen hunting around dusk or dawn, kestrels will hunt during daylight hours.

Males and females can be easily identified; females are brown all over, while males have blue grey heads and wing feathers.

The Latin word *falco* means sickle, and refers to the sickle-shaped talons of falcons and hawks. *Tinnunculus* means shrill – relating to the high-pitched call of the kestrel.

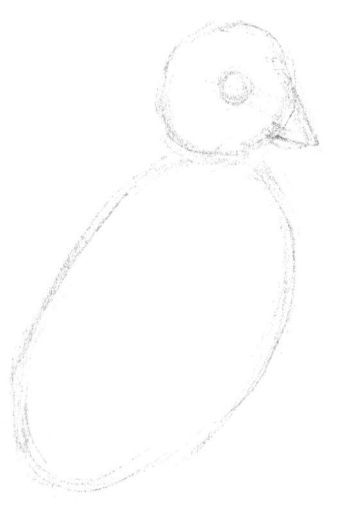

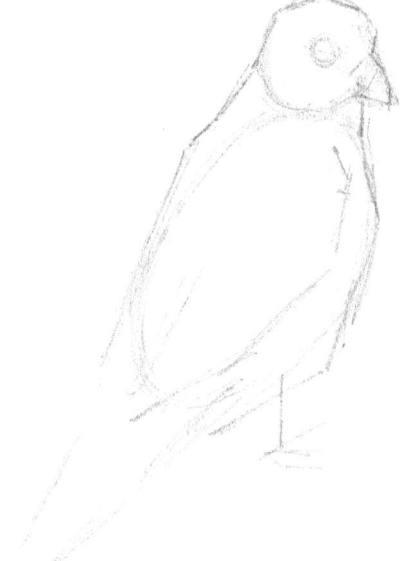

STEP 1

Begin as usual with the now familiar bird shapes; circle for the head and oval for the body. The beak is represented with a short triangle; to be shaped into a hooked beak later. At this stage, you can also draw a line midway through the circle at an angle appropriate for the angle of the head.

STEP 2

Straight lines and angles will connect the shapes and add strength to the curves in the circle and oval. A couple of straight lines will show the basic angle and length of the tail feathers. Position the eye along the line dividing the circle at this stage.

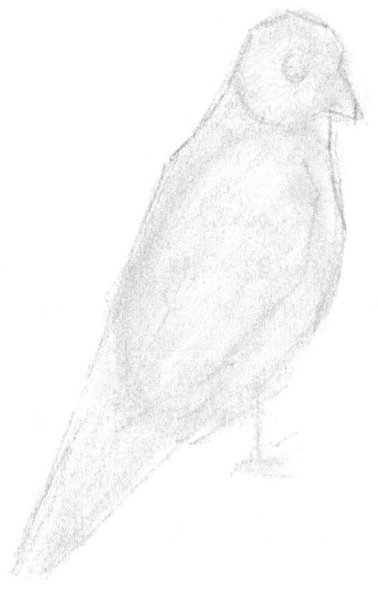

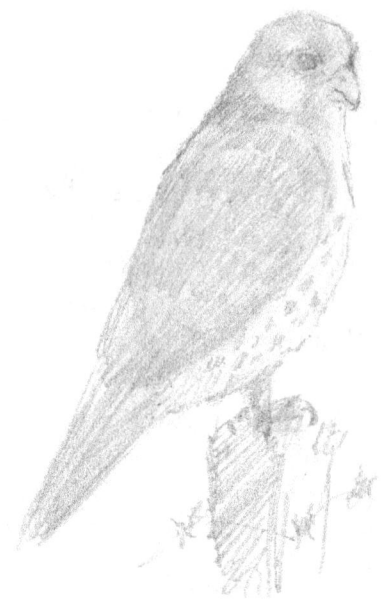

STEP 3

Using the side of your pencil, add the mid grey base tone over the whole bird; (pale areas, such as the chest will be lifted out later). Keep the hatched lines close together for a smoother overall tone when you blend with the tortillon or paper towel.

STEP 4

Begin adding texture to the wing by creating blocks of hatched shading from short covert feathers down to longer primary feathers. Use longer hatch strokes for the tail feathers. Use the kneadable eraser to 'clean up' the chest area, then sketch in the markings on the chest feathers.
Sketch in the feet and soften the texture slightly with the tortillon. Add in the talons, but keep them sharp.
Shape the beak so that the larger upper mandible has the sickle-shaped hook and add in the nostril.
Strengthen the shape of the eye and add in the upper and lower rims and the slightly darker feathers around the eye.
If you want to, you can sketch in a gatepost for the kestrel to perch on, adding some barbed wire for additional interesting texture.

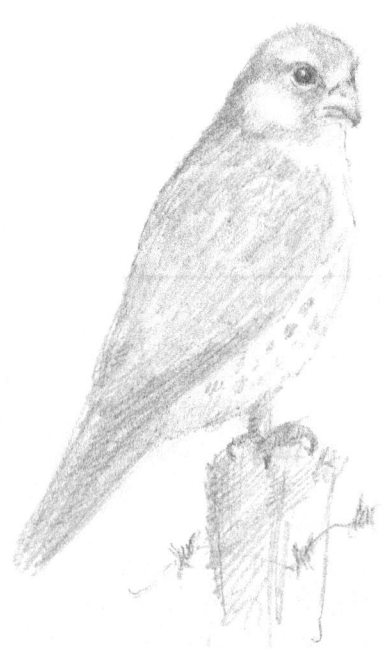

STEP 5

Sharpen and darken the important features, such as the eye, along with the surrounding markings and the beak.
Lift out the final highlights around the head with the kneadable eraser. You can also add a little definition to the wing feathers with the eraser.

A LITTLE BIRD TOLD ME...

Feel free to add some background and/or embellishments to fill out your sketch.
You can perhaps extend the barbed wire on the post to form a kind of frame around your kestrel.

ADDITIONAL BIRD OF PREY IMAGES

BUZZARD

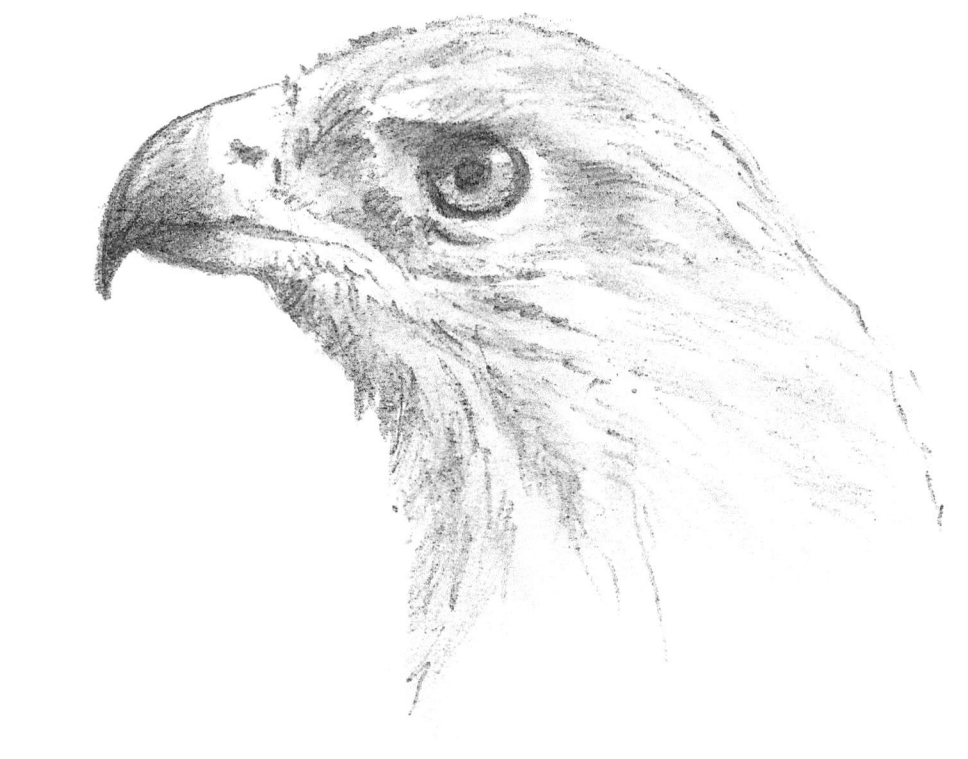

LITTLE OWL

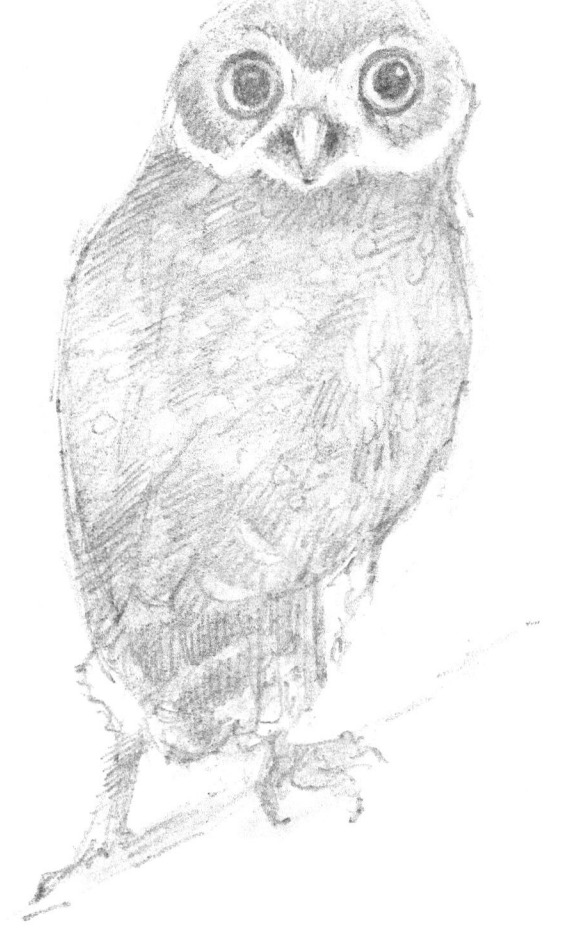

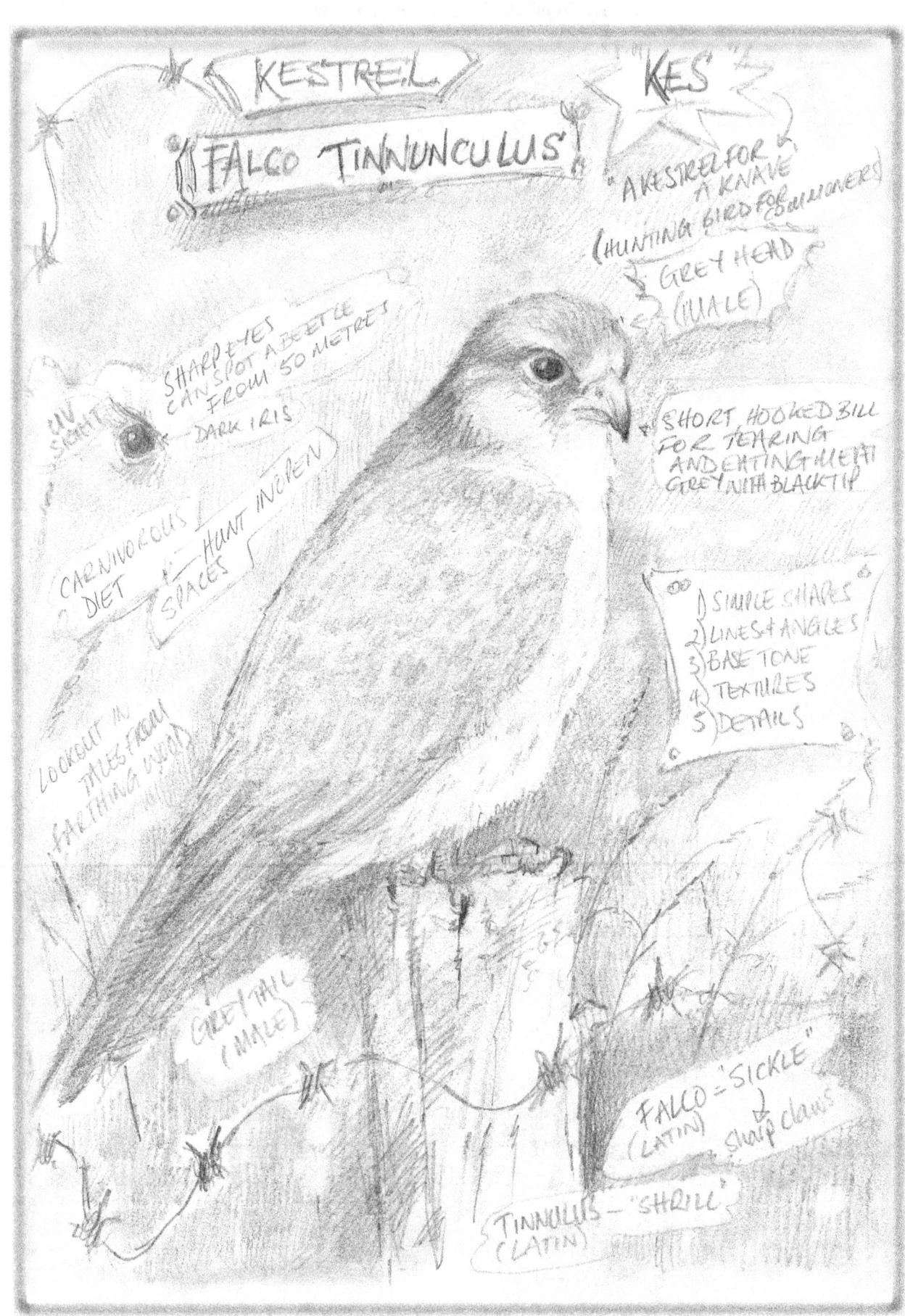

KESTREL   "KES"

FALCO TINNUNCULUS

"A KESTREL FOR
A KNAVE"
(HUNTING BIRD FOR COMMONERS)

GREY HEAD
(MALE)

SHARP EYES
CAN SPOT A BEETLE
FROM 50 METRES

UV SIGHT

DARK IRIS

SHORT HOOKED BILL
FOR TEARING
AND EATING MEAT
GREY WITH BLACK TIP

CARNIVOROUS DIET — HUNT IN OPEN SPACES

1) SIMPLE SHAPES
2) LINES & ANGLES
3) BASE TONE
4) TEXTURES
5) DETAILS

LOOKOUT IN TALLEST TREES FARTHING BIRD

GREY TAIL (MALE)

FALCO = "SICKLE"
(LATIN)
SHARP CLAWS

TINNULUS — "SHRILL"
(LATIN)

31

CHAPTER 6

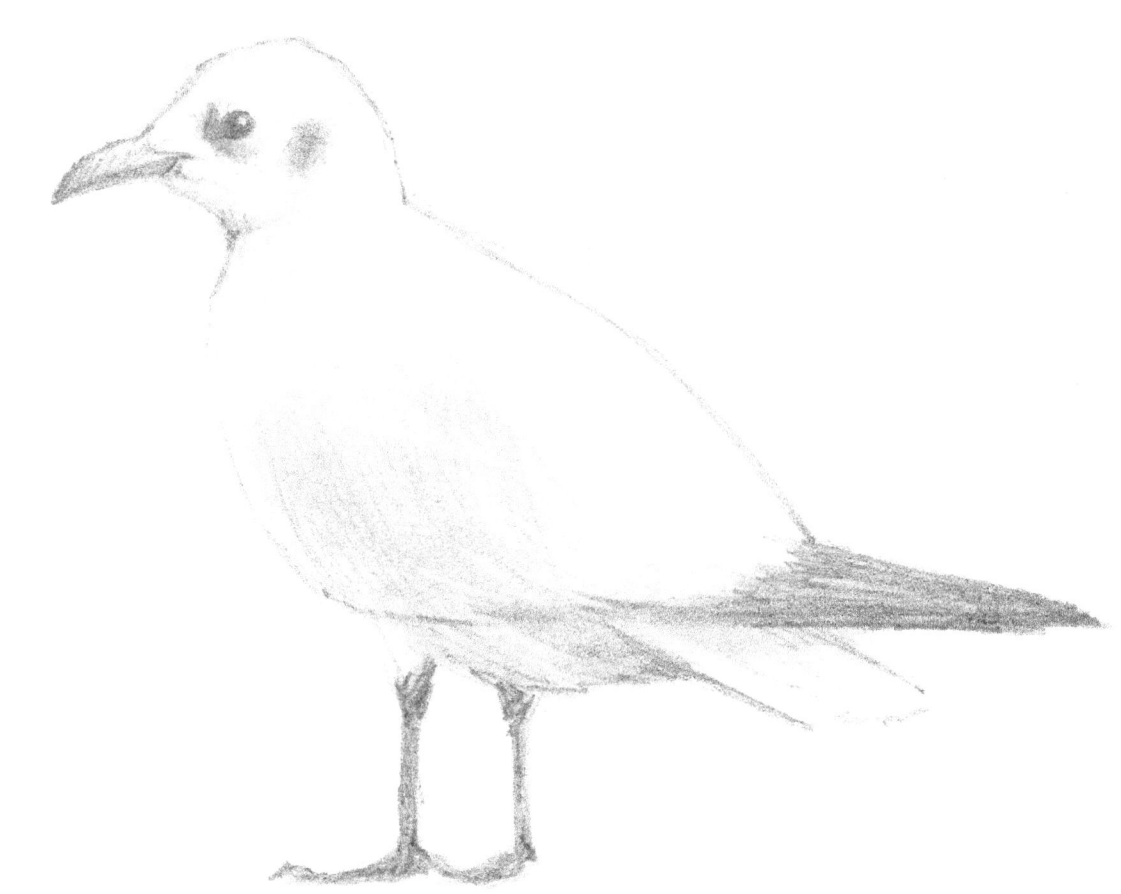

SEABIRDS

SEABIRDS

When the word 'seabird' is mentioned, the image that is most likely to be conjured up is a seagull.

Of course, there are other seabirds around our coastline of all shapes and sizes; puffins, terns, shags and any number of gulls. In recent years, largely due to environmental changes, some species, including cormorants and a number of gull species have adapted to life away from the sea, but are still regarded as seabirds.

Gulls in particular can be quite characterful birds; for example the herring gull, the largest of all, infamous seaside pirate and plunderer of chips, sandwiches and ice creams.

Gulls that spend some of their lives around inland waterways and landfill sites can also be as raucous as their seaside cousins.

ESSENTIAL FEATURES

Beak/Bill

As you might imagine, seabirds' beaks are multi-functional tools, often with a 'nail' or hook at the end, used for anything from prying molluscs from crevices to stealing chips.

Feet

Like their waterfowl counterparts (ducks geese and swans), seabirds also have webbed feet, reagardless of whether they live mostly out of water or not. The webbing is attached between the first and second and the second and third toes.

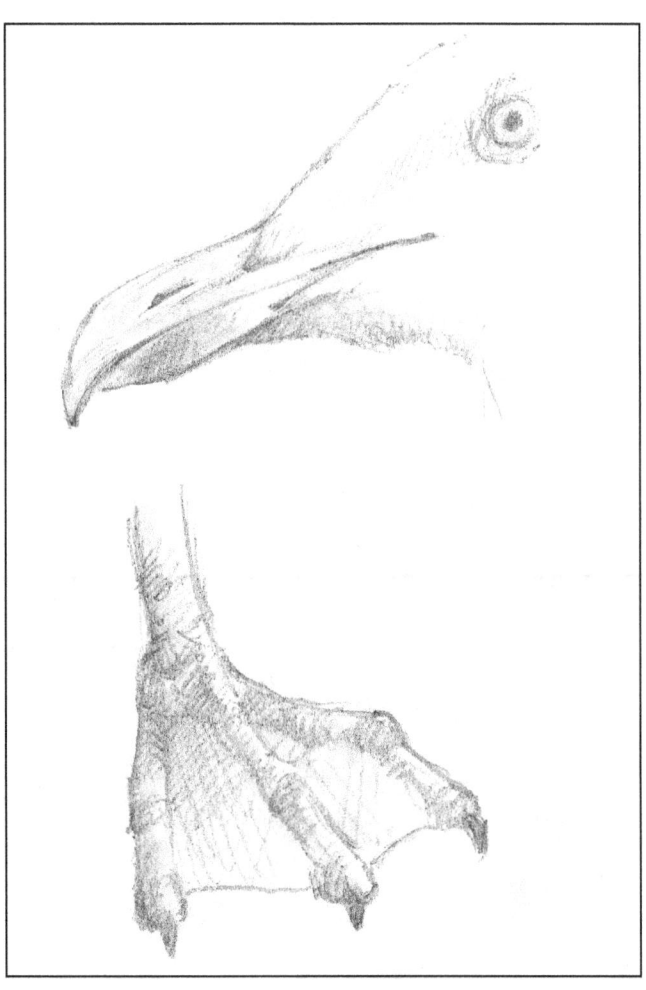

PROJECT

Black-headed gull *(chroicocephalus ridibundus)*

The black-headed gull is the smallest of the common gulls. Although it can be seen in some coastal areas, the black-headed gull is a fairly common site around inland waterways, lakes and marshes.

The black-headed gull has a rather noisy, laughter like cry, and the Latin part of its name – *ridibundus* – means 'laughing'. The first part of its name – *chroicocephalus* – is Greek for 'coloured head'.

The strange thing about this bird is that it only has a distinctive black or dark brown head in the summer. In the autumn, the plumage around the head changes to mostly white, with just a small patch of black plumage over the ears.

For this project, the black-headed gull is in its winter finery.

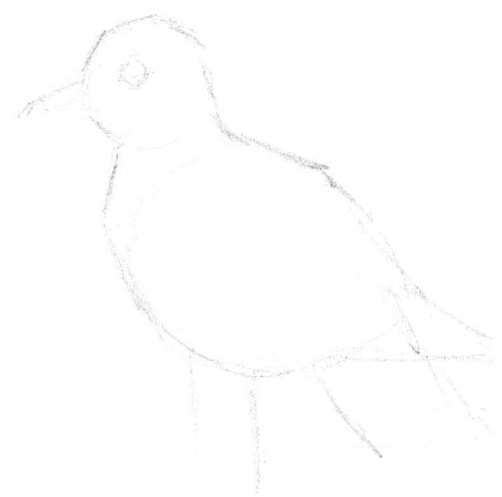

STEP 1

As you begin with the basic shapes, make sure to leave a gap between the circle and the oval to allow for the gull's neck. The basic beak shape is a longer, thinner triangle than usual.

STEP 2

Round off the curves of the head and body with straight lines, looking for those all-important angles that will make your sketch stronger and more dynamic. Add in the shape of the wing, tail feathers and upper part of the legs. Remember to keep it simple at this stage.

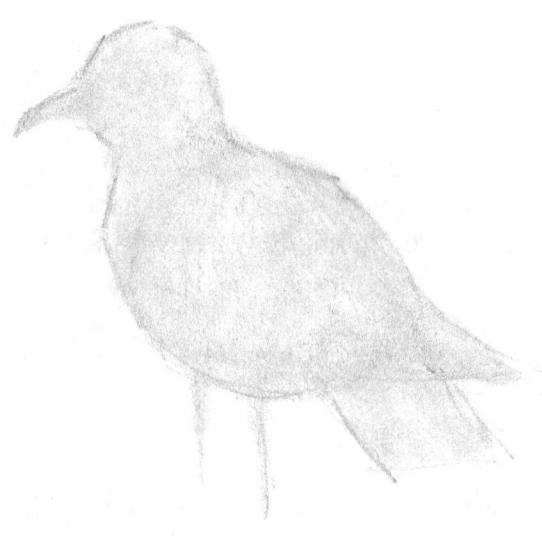

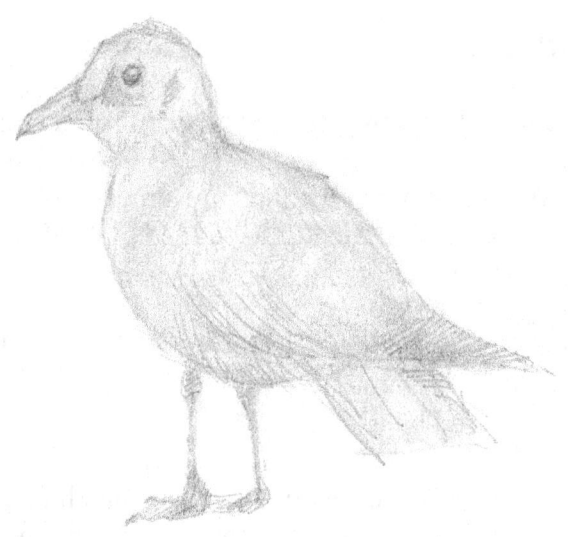

STEP 3

Add in the mid grey base layer, using the side of your pencil and the tortillon. Remember that the closer your hatched lines, the smoother the base tone will be.

STEP 4

Begin to add the details. You won't have to worry too much about feather texture in this sketch, as the plumage is mostly white. Concentrate instead on the eye, beak and feet. If you place the reflection towards the back of the gull's eye, you will give it that mischievous look.

Make sure the primary wing feathers have a suitably dark tone, then use the kneadable eraser to lift out areas of white plumage and to suggest some flight feathers – the wing will be left grey from the initial base tone. Adding some darker shading in the background will help the white plumage to be more visible.

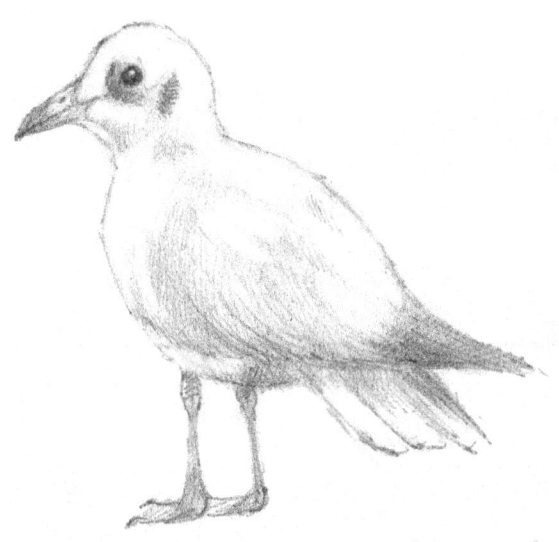

STEP 5

Finally, make sure the important features – eyes and beak are sharper and stronger in tone so they become the main focus of your sketch.

A LITTLE BIRD TOLD ME...

In my finished sketch, I have embellished the background with some stormy-looking swirls, lifted out with the eraser, as gulls are said to be 'harbingers of the storm'. I've also included a sketch remarque of the same bird in its summer plumage. You can, of course, add as much or as little as you want to your own sketch, as with all the step by step projects in this book.

PUFFIN

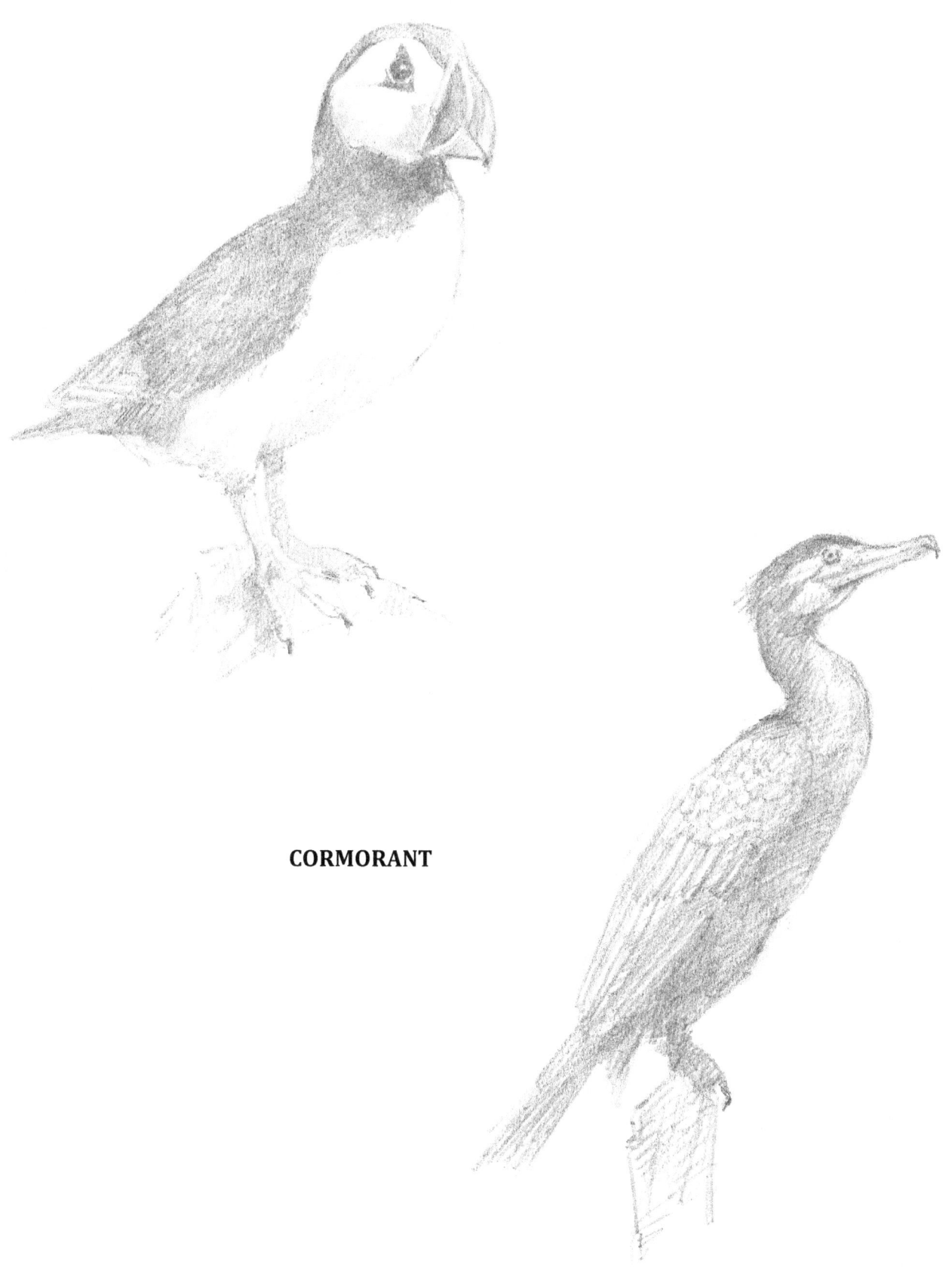

CORMORANT

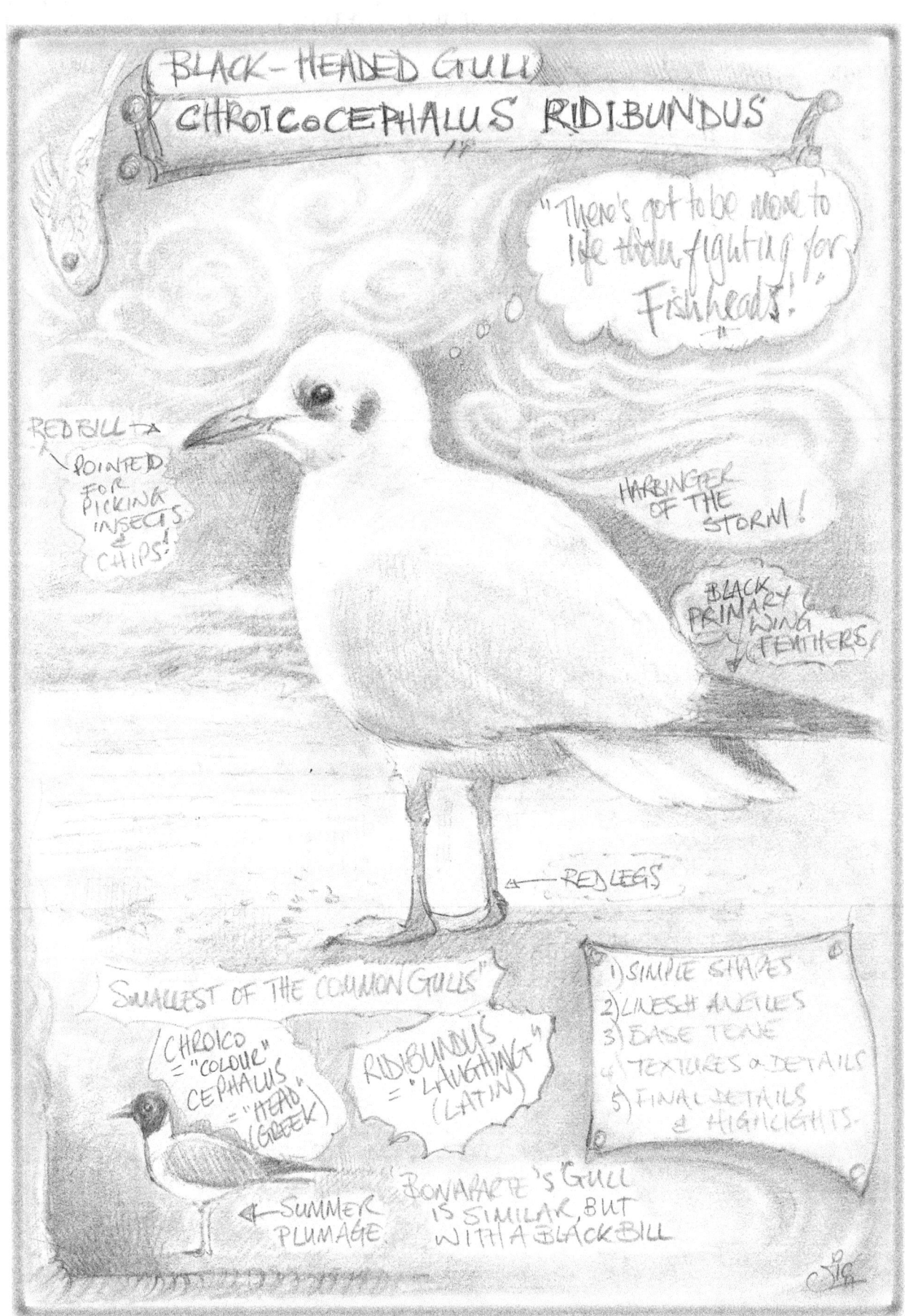

AFTERWARD

I hope you've enjoyed this book and learned something about my sketching technique.

Of course, a book like this can only hope to cover a very small proportion of the vast number of bird species. However, by varying the basic shapes – mainly head, body, beak and feet – I am confident that you will be able to sketch any bird, from the commonly seen to the more exotic.

For information and details about the workshops and courses I run online, which are available to anyone in the world, visit mywebsite.

www.vicbearcroft.co.uk

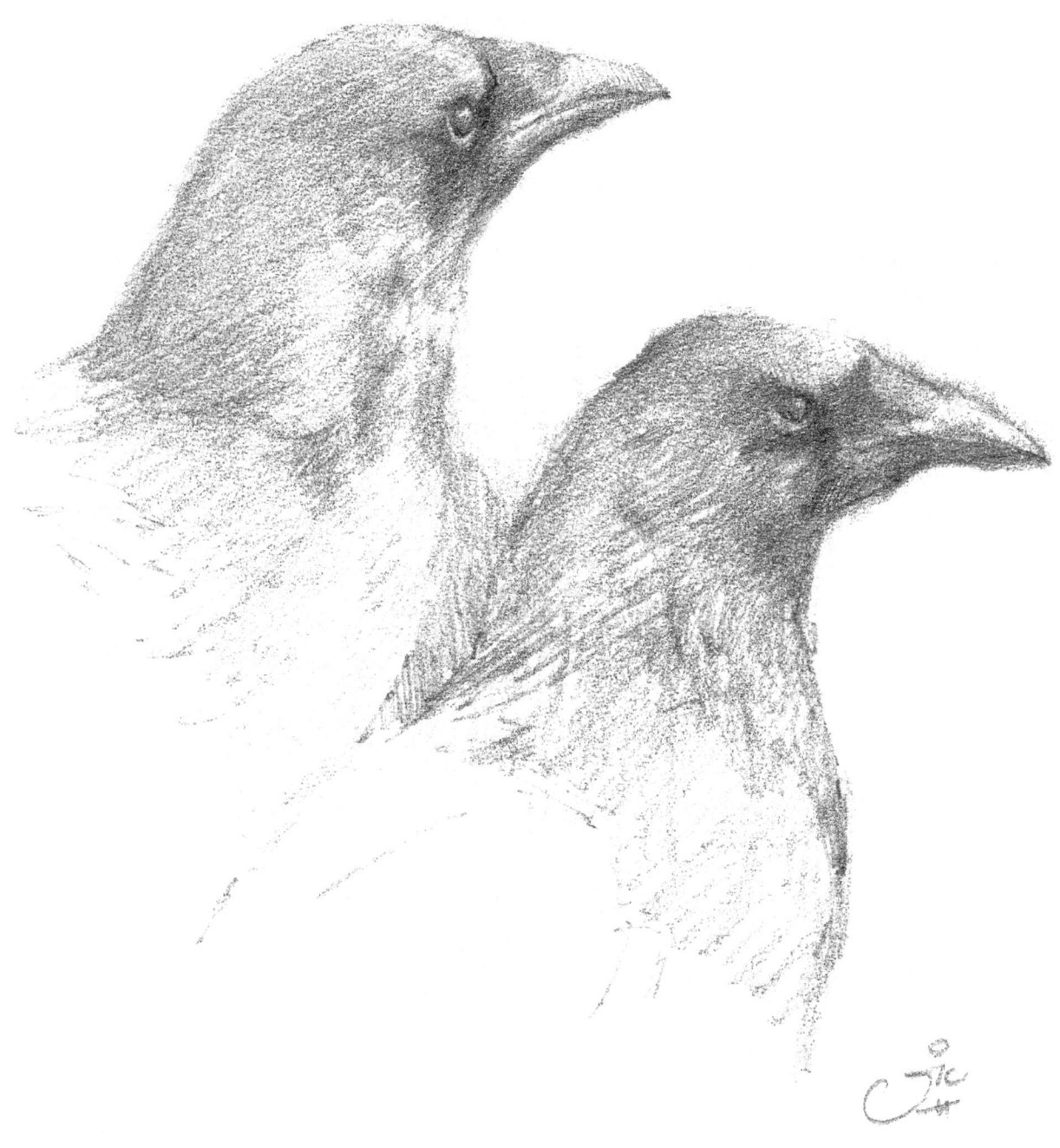

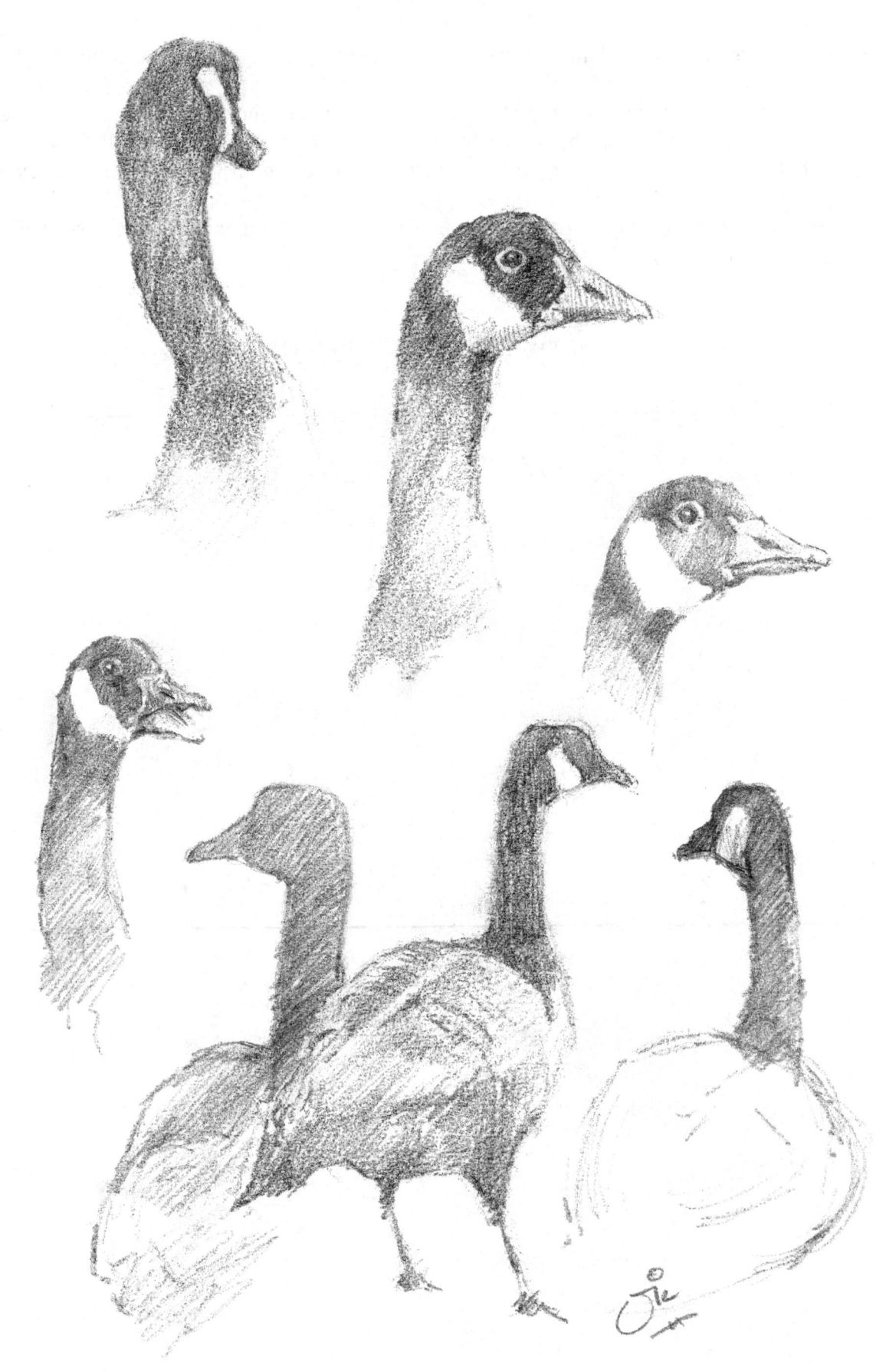

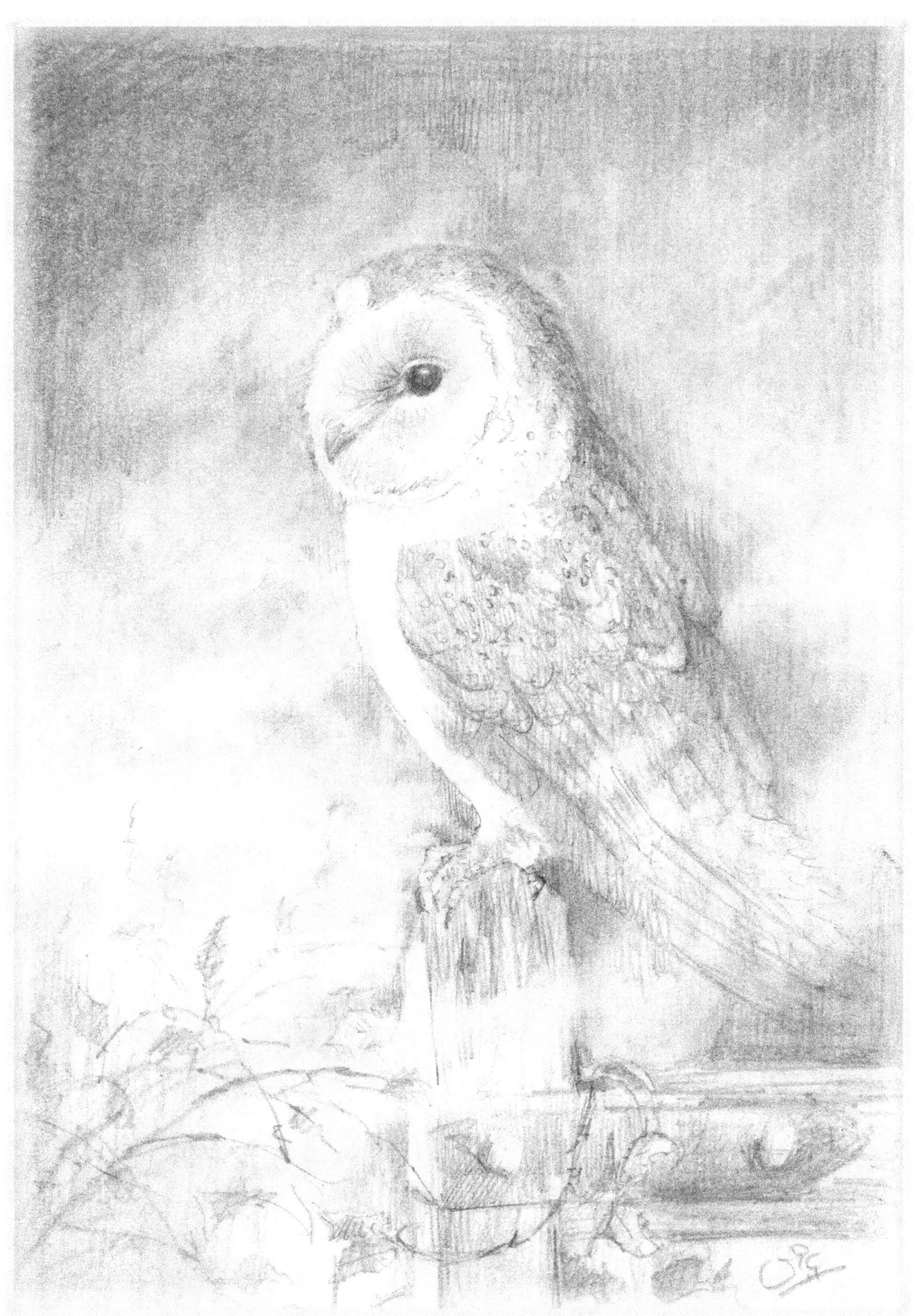

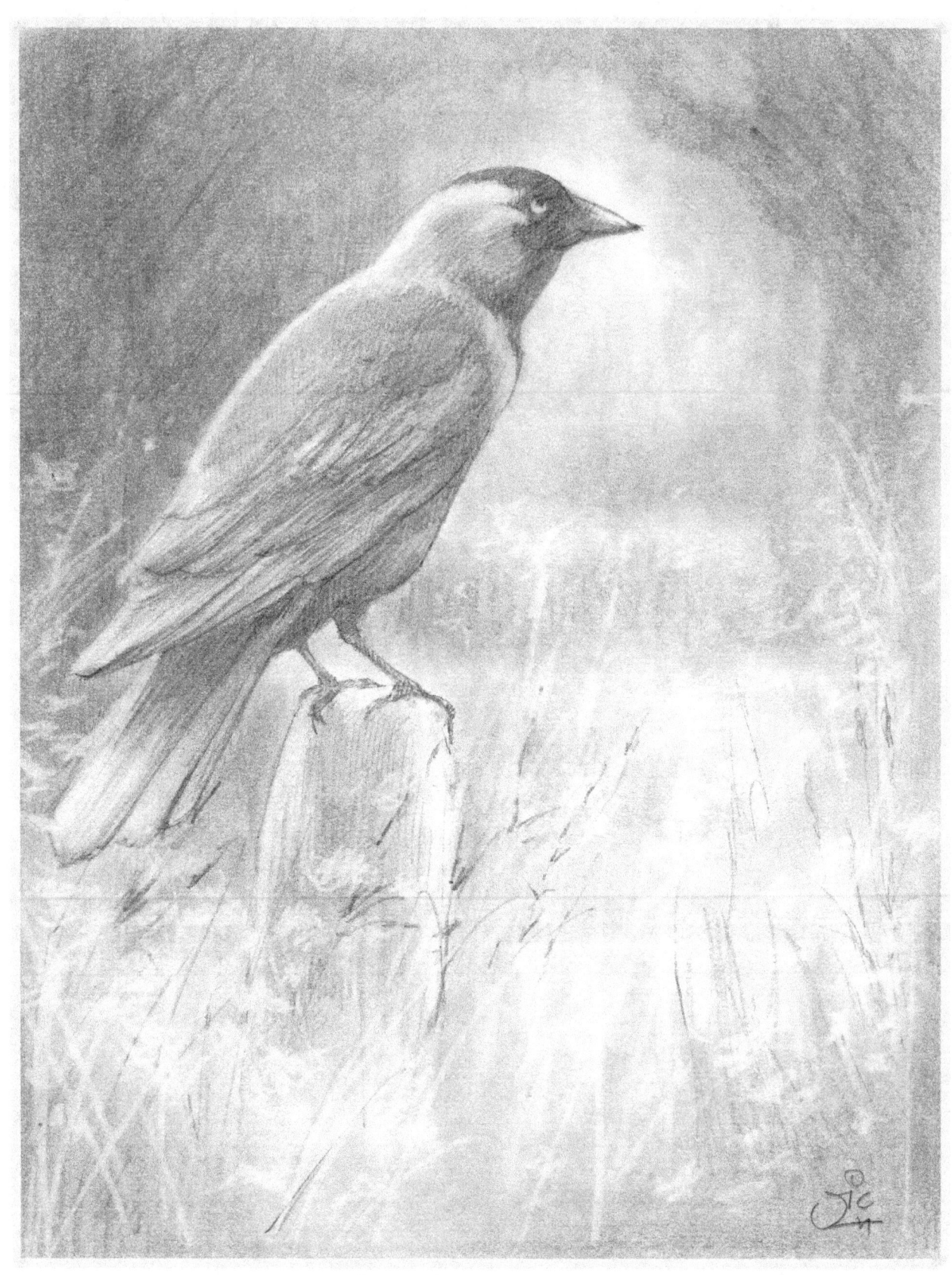

41

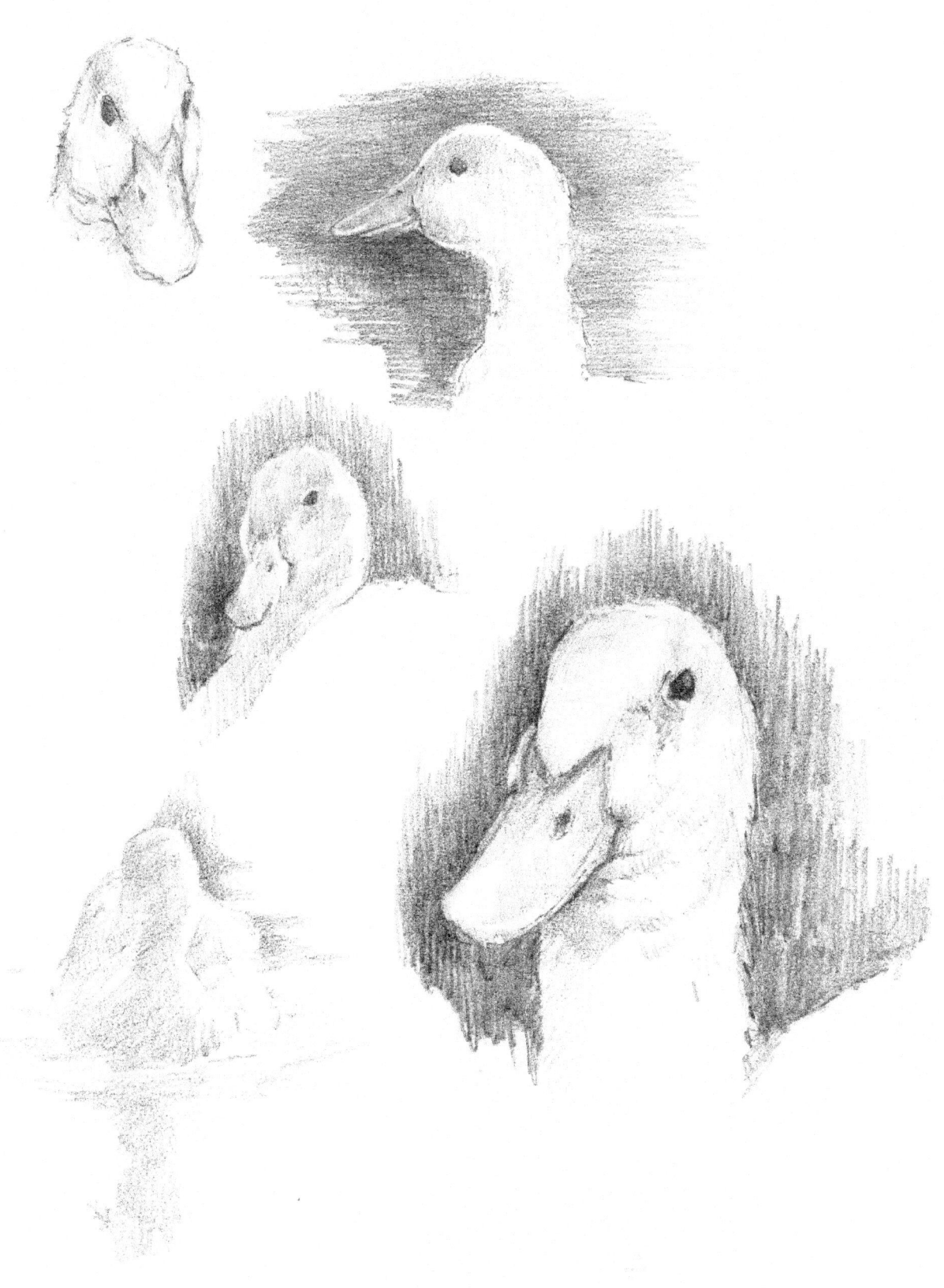

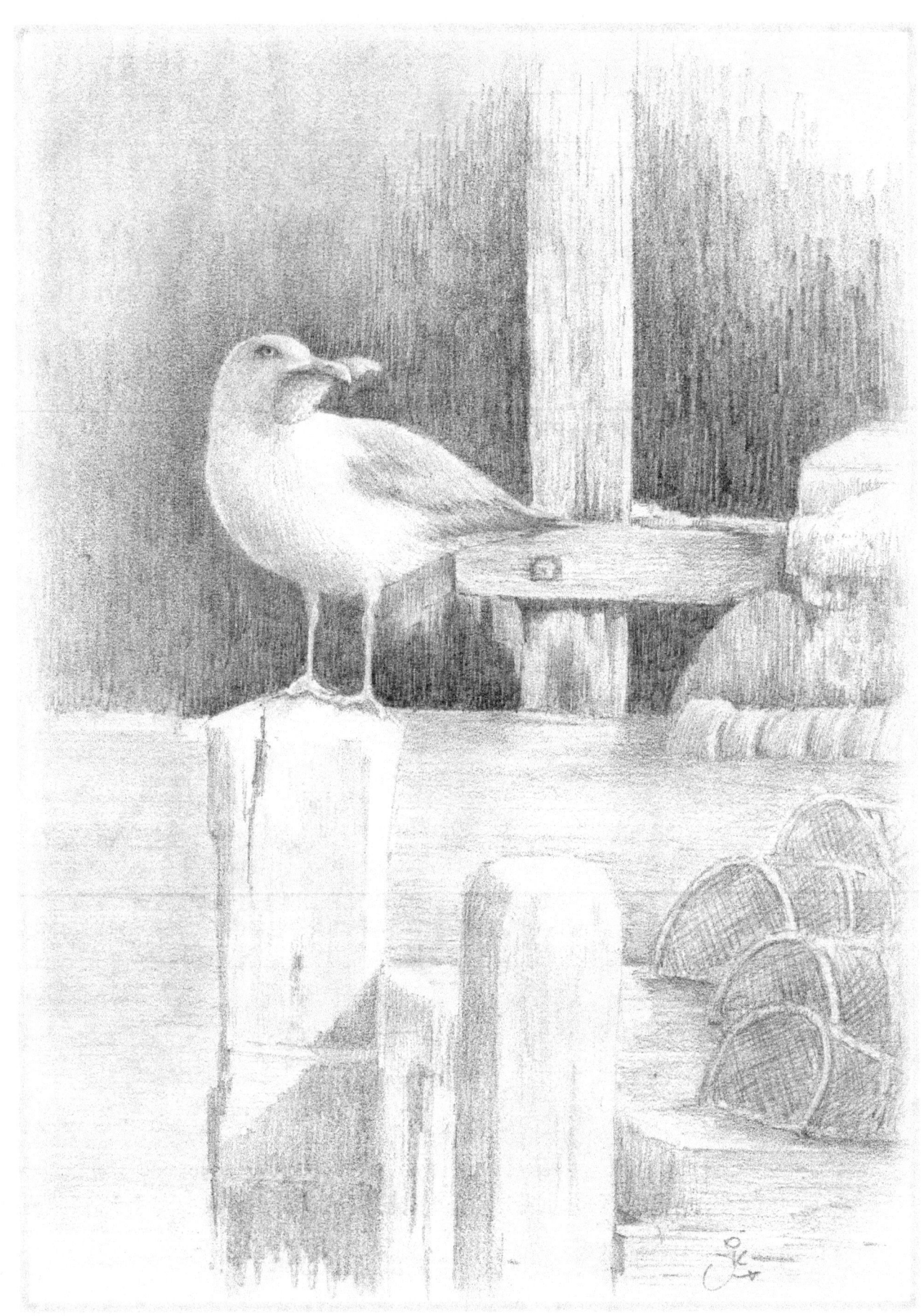